Apocalypse
and other poems
ERNESTO
CARDENAL

ALSO BY ERNESTO CARDENAL

In Cuba

Apocalypse and other poems

ERNESTO CARDENAL

Edited and selected by Robert Pring-Mill and Donald D. Walsh, with an introduction by Robert Pring-Mill

Translations by Thomas Merton, Kenneth Rexroth and Mireya Jaimes-Freyre, and the editors

A NEW DIRECTIONS BOOK

ACKNOWLEDGMENTS
Grateful acknowledgment is made to the editors and publishers of books and magazines in which some of the translations in this volume originally appeared: *America* (Copyright © 1975 by America Press, Inc.; reprinted by permission), *Emblems of a Season of Fury* by Thomas Merton (New Directions: Copyright © 1961, 1962, 1963 by The Abbey of Gethsemani, Inc.), *The Nation, New Catholic World, New Directions in Prose and Poetry,* and *Pax.*

Special thanks are due to the editors and publishers of the following books, in which poems by Ernesto Cardenal included in this volume appear in other translations: *Homage to the American Indians* (The Johns Hopkins University Press; Translation Copyright © 1973 by The Johns Hopkins University Press; used by permission), *Marilyn Monroe and Other Poems* (Search Press, London; used by permission), *The Psalms of Struggle and Liberation* (Herder and Herder; used by permission of The Seabury Press).

Library of Congress Cataloging in Publication Data

Cardenal, Ernesto.
  Apocalypse, and other poems.
  (A New Directions Book)
  I. Title.
PQ7519.C34A25   1977   861   77–7280
ISBN 0–8112–0661–0
ISBN 0–8112–0662–9 pbk.

New Directions Books are published for James Laughlin
by New Directions Publishing Corporation,
333 Sixth Avenue, New York 10014

CONTENTS

PREFACE

As Robert Pring-Mill makes clear in his introduction, Ernesto Cardenal is not only a great poet but a committed poet, an activist poet, a Marxist poet, a man who finds no contradiction between his commitment to the priesthood and his commitment to freedom and social justice and human dignity.

Unfortunately, respect for freedom and social justice and human dignity cannot be taken for granted in Latin America. These ideals must be fought for, and Cardenal fights, from his parish in Nicaragua, from the pages of his poetry, and from the platform in his frequent appearances in Latin America and in the United States.

The first work of Cardenal that I read was *En Cuba,* a report on a three-month visit in 1970. It was perceptive and realistic reporting of the virtues and defects of Castro's Cuba by a proud leftwinger. I was happy to translate it for New Directions.

I next read his *Viaje a Nueva York,* a documentary poem about a trip that he made here in 1973. (It will be part of a projected New Directions volume of Cardenal poetry, to be entitled *Zero Hour and Other Documentary Poems.*)

Cardenal is a relatively young man, in his early fifties, and he is still vigorously creative. His most recent book to appear in English is *The Gospel in Solentiname* (Orbis Books, 1976), a series of the vocal (and sometimes highly vocal) reactions to the Sunday Gospel lessons made by members of Father Cardenal's parish at Our Lady of Solentiname on Lake Nicaragua.

Some of my own translations in this volume were previously published in *America, London Magazine,* and *The Nation.* Permission to reprint them is hereby gratefully acknowledged.

Most people who know Cardenal are convinced that he is a saint; others are equally convinced that he is the devil in priestly disguise. I am one of the "most people," and I hope that this volume will make readers of it join the majority.

Madison, Conn.   D. D. W.

INTRODUCTION

Ernesto Cardenal is a Spanish-American poet who speaks with a Third World voice. Till recently, few people in the First World really "listened" to things that Third World writers had to say. If heard at all, they were heard as one hears the sea grumbling on a beach, or given the attention one gives background music during conversation. Yet the Third World's best writers should command a better hearing; not just for what they say about their own world, but also for the things they tell us about ours.

Cardenal, a Nicaraguan born in 1925, is a deeply committed poet and a revolutionary Roman Catholic priest. This double commitment has been partly shaped by the nature of his country: its politics, social structure, and geography—all remote from those with which most First World people are familiar. But particular situations may prompt a writer to form general views which are applicable to other sets of circumstances, and Cardenal—nurtured in the Nicaraguan context of life under a typical Latin American dictatorship—has been led by his own experience not only at home but also in the States to question many of the values of Western society.

His poems deserve attention both for the ideas expressed (whether one agrees with these or not) and for their intrinsic poetic merit. The ideas themselves are generally simple, but the poetic artifact is often complex: deft in its manipulation of techniques, and many-layered in meaning. The obvious layer is immediately clear, conveyed with singular economy of means in a language lean and spare yet sonorous, and handled with meticulous precision. If asked to classify him (always a dangerous thing) one would have to label Cardenal a "protest poet," but the label carries overtones of stridency—and of unsubtlety—which rarely fit the poetry in this collection. Yet the tag suits his purpose, and it situates him in a living Latin American tradition, which relates to recurring situations in time-honored ways.

Given the conditions of poverty under which most people live in Latin American countries, and the political structures which circumscribe their lives, it is no surprise that the growth of social and political awareness has produced so much protest poetry since the mid-1940s.

Many other genres display social concern, with authors conscious of a moral duty to act as guide and conscience of their people, but the poet has a special function: poems are more memorable (in both senses) than novels, tracts, or treatises. Poems can also operate at different levels, reaching different sectors of society.

The committed poet exploits all the rhetorical techniques employed in such traditional genres as lyric, epic, tragic, comic, or satirical verse, but in the service of a strictly twentieth-century "message." Aimed at rousing and persuading readers, his poetry is necessarily "rhetorical" in the good sense of the word—though the bad sense also fits poor protest poetry—using tried means to modern ends, and speaking to an audience in tune with its conventions. Cardenal belongs to this tradition, but he has also modified it: the finest committed poet of the generation following that of Neruda (1904–73), his own innovations are today a major influence on younger poets. His adult poems all show a deep sense of human involvement, but in the major part of his work—certainly in the bulk of the poems in this collection—his social criticism is the more powerful for using various "modes of indirection."

Cardenal's commitment has been specifically Christian since 1956, and after his ordination to the Catholic priesthood nine years later he founded a small community—"more of a commune, really" (as he put it) "but *comuna* wasn't yet a current word in American Spanish"—on a remote tropical island in Lake Nicaragua, called Mancarrón. There he still works and writes. The setting is idyllic but the life is fairly hard, basically that of the Nicaraguan *campesino*—which is what most members of his loose-knit foundation are—though with the addition of meditation, prayer, and study. Its "first rule is that there are no formal rules," says Cardenal, nor any of the ritual of traditional monasticism. But there is a folk-mass on Sundays, to which dozens of *campesinos* from other islands in the Solentiname Archipelago come in open boats.

The community is called Our Lady of Solentiname, after the islands, and the special kind of revolutionary Pauline Christianity which it follows and its founder teaches (much influenced by the "theology of liberation") exerts great influence among progressive Catholics in many parts of Latin America, forming one particular wing—far out on the Left—of the general movement of *concientización, i.e.* the promotion of socioreligious awareness throughout society, from the grassroots up. Its teaching grows and develops partly in Cardenal's own writings, and partly through discussion of the social relevance of Scripture: a discussion in which the humblest *campesino* joins.* The existence of such a community is irksome to the Nicaraguan government, yet its prestige abroad is such that it is tolerated. For obvious reasons, few of the poet's works have appeared in his own country, though they have achieved considerable circulation underground.

Cardenal's poetry, and not his prose, concerns us here. This brief essay outlines his evolution as a poet, providing a context for an introductory selection of his poems. The earliest of these, "Drake in the Southern Sea," belongs to the late 1940s, while the most recent ("The Arrival" and "Condensations") date from late 1973. Unlike most Latin American poets, Cardenal operates within a tradition which includes an English-language strand. Since the early 1930s, Nicaraguan poetry has been deeply influenced by North American writers, initially thanks to José Coronel Urtecho (b.1906), who introduced the works of Pound, Eliot, Robinson Jeffers, William Carlos Williams, Frost, and Sandburg to his compatriots.

Coronel later published a *Panorama y antología de la poesía norteamericana,* and Cardenal and he began a greatly enlarged version in the 1950s, with the younger man translating works by poets such as Rolfe Humphries, Ginsberg, Rexroth, Josephine Miles, Randall Jarrell, Thomas Merton, James Laughlin, Robert Lowell, Lawrence Ferlinghetti, William Everson (Brother Antoninus), Denise Levertov, Philip Lamantia, John Ashbery, Philip Whalen, and Gary Snyder. Merton's was a special case, and Cardenal published a whole book of translations of his poetry in 1961, but Merton's influence on Cardenal was less importantly poetic than it was spiritual: Our Lady of Solentiname is not just a foundation after Merton's heart but the fruit of plans for a community the two had often discussed.

In poetry, Cardenal regards Ezra Pound as the greatest influence on his work. Initially, it helped him escape the dominance of Neruda and Rubén Darío (1867–1916)—the latter the greatest Nicaraguan poet, whose *modernista* mode inevitably exerted a not wholly beneficial influence on all later Nicaraguan poets. The influence of Darío and Neruda is obvious in the poems Cardenal wrote at high school, and during his student years in Mexico (1943–47)—poetry which he has since discarded. He came under Pound's poetic influence when he attended Columbia University from 1947 to 1949—years when Merton's

---

* For a first selection of such discussions, see *The Gospel in Solentiname,* edited by Cardenal and translated by Donald D. Walsh (Orbis Books, 1976). Cardenal today regards this on-going project as the most important part of his religious mission.

early spiritual works were appearing, of which the young Nicaraguan became an avid reader.

Pound's influence affects Cardenal's poetry in various ways at different times, but two Poundian features are present throughout the poems he keeps in print. The first is the exclusion of subjective elements, for which he and Coronel coined the name *exteriorismo* in the mid-1950s. Their joint translation of Pound's famous "A Few Don'ts" (published as *Varios "No"* in 1961) became a retrospective *exteriorista* manifesto. The second is the use of nonpoetic sources: chronicles, historical documents, anthropological reports, economic digests, articles in magazines, press-cuttings—even advertisements.

Both are already present in "Drake in the Southern Sea" (printed here in a version by Thomas Merton). In such a case, the precise source scarcely matters. In others, part of the meaning may lie in the interaction between poem and source, as in Cardenal's up-dated psalms or in "Apocalypse"—the title poem of this collection. At times, quotations are explicit and the source is named. Even when one might not suspect its existence, there is usually some written antecedent, e.g. "Above the Rain-Soaked Track" (an early poem, without a social relevance), although it sounds like direct observation, was inspired by a French traveler's account of Central America.

His earliest committed poetry was very different from this lush tropical vignette, but it shows the same careful use of minor echoes, and the same extreme economy of statement. Fascinated by the terseness of Pound's translations from the classics, Cardenal began writing epigrams. The earliest were love poems, but they soon became political. Nicaragua had been run by a dictator, Anastasio ("Tacho") Somoza, since the American marines withdrew in 1932. The young poet became involved in revolutionary politics, and his anonymous abrasive satires circulated underground, passing "from hand to hand, in manuscript or mimeograph" (No. 35). In April 1954, he was involved in an abortive plot. Most of the leaders were captured, and slaughtered after savage torture—Somoza's son (the "Tachito" of No. 26, who still rules Nicaragua) allegedly taking part in their interrogation. Cardenal only just managed to escape, and No. 30 is an epitaph for one of his closest friends among the leaders killed. The resurrection motif, there given a purely revolutionary relevance, became one of the poet's favorite themes, endowed with multiple meanings.

From 1954 to 1956, Cardenal spent much time translating Latin epigrammatists and writing his first "documentary" poem—too long for inclusion here—called *Hora O* ("Zero Hour"), today a revolutionary classic. In 1956, "Tacho" Somoza was killed; soon afterward, Cardenal experienced his spiritual conversion. This led him both to abjure the use of violence and to join the Trappist noviciate at Gethsemani, where he discovered—to his great delight—that Merton was the novice-master. "NNW" was one of the last poems he wrote before he went off to Kentucky.

Cardenal's health, never very strong, gave way, and after two years at Gethsemani he moved—on Merton's advice—to the Benedictine priory at Cuernavaca (August 1959) to continue his studies for the priesthood, completing these in the seminary of La Ceja (Colombia) from 1961 to 1965. At Gethsemani, his creative writing had been deliberately restricted, but his spiritual notebook subsequently formed the basis of a book of mystical reflections—on love as the underlying matrix of existence—frequently reflected in his later poetry, e.g. in the epithalamium which ends "Apocalypse," or in the last poem in this volume.

Other jottings made in Gethsemani were reworked at Cuernavaca to produce the thirty-one tightly disciplined poems of *Gethsemani, Ky.*: "utterly simple poetic sketches," in Merton's phrase, exhibiting the same combination of "purity and sophistication we find in the Chinese masters of the T'ang dynasty." Merton translated twelve of them: the eleven published in his *Emblems of a Season of Fury* (1963)—two of which are given here—and "Like Empty Beer Cans," which has not previously appeared in print. Others, such as "The Marmots in Their Burrows," recorded the Nicaraguan's fascination with the northern shift from winter into spring, using the "rebirth" of hibernating animals as a "figure" of Resurrection all the more effective for not being spelled out.

Such poems leave their spiritual message unstated—almost enigmatic. This technique of understatement is very un-Spanish, but Cardenal carried it over into his social poetry to good effect. It characterizes the book-length epic *El estrecho dudoso* ("The Doubtful Passage," unrepresented here), also written in Cuernavaca. This ostensibly deals with the history of Central America, from the coming of the Spaniards down to the destruction of Nicaragua's León Viejo by volcanic action in 1609, but handles its historical material in such a way that it becomes an oblique commentary on the modern period. Thus Pedrarias—first "exploiter" of Nicaragua—is patently a "figure" of Somoza. The copious documentary material is all carefully reworked, with much cross-cutting between sources, frequently weaving direct quotations into the free-verse structure as in Pound's *Cantos*.

Similarly, Cardenal's numerous poems on the Indian past of the Americas* are really all critiques of aspects of the modern world. The first, "The Lost Cities," was also written during that highly productive year and a half at Cuernavaca. About the ancient Maya, it does depend on serious archaeological studies, but its first inspiration was an article from *Life,* pinned up on the noviciate noticeboard back in Gethsemani by Merton, and Cardenal attributes the burgeoning of his interest in Amerindian themes to Merton's influence. This poem is colored by the Mayan vision of time as cyclical: time past thus takes on an intensified relevance to time present, without the need to spell this meaning out at length.

The later Amerindian poems use similar modes of indirection, but they present their elements discontinuously, as in "Katún 11 Ahau" (written during the early years of the Solentiname commune). The sustained approach of "The Lost Cities" can, however, help the reader to appreciate the basic interplay of attitudes, and hence to follow its workings when it reappears in the more "cinematographic" poems—whose sequences of discontinuous images have been carefully built up, like a film in the cutting room, when the constituent parts were variously assembled in successive drafts until the poet arrived at the "right" order.

During his last years at La Ceja, Cardenal's interest in Amerindian themes spread to the Incas, to ancient Mexico, and finally to the more "primitive" cultures—past and present—whose values appealed to him with peculiar intensity as the plans for his own "primitive" Christian outpost grew toward fruition. After his ordination, but before going to Mancarrón to clear the jungle and start building the first hut, he went back to the States to see Merton, and also visited the Pueblo Indians. This contact led to interest in Red Indian cultures, and the seventeen poems of *Homenaje a los indios americanos* (1970)† include four poems on Red Indian themes, to which he later added "Recordings of the Sacred Pipe." Throughout these poems one finds implicit criticism of modern socioeconomic structures, and also of militarism—the early Maya are particularly praised because "There are no names of generals on the stelae." But after "The Lost Cities," he dealt with two different kinds of subject, in quite different ways, before continuing the cycle of Amerindian poems.

A more direct critique of modern values came in *Oración por*

* See *Homage to the American Indian,* translated by Monique and Carlos Altschul (The Johns Hopkins University Press, 1973).

† A fifteen-poem edition had appeared in Nicaragua in 1969.

Marilyn Monroe y otros poemas (1965), nine of whose twelve poems—including "Managua 6:30 P.M." and "Unrighteous Mammon"—were written before he moved from Cuernavaca to La Ceja. Most items in this slim collection involve a meditation on modern life, or on one of its "representative" events or features, such as a gangster killing or an air crash, the glossiness of tourist propaganda, or the death of Marilyn Monroe. Contemplation of the insecurities and falsities of Western life embodies criticism of the affluent society, whose values are seen in the ethos of mass advertising or sensationalist reportage. The actual "Prayer for Marilyn Monroe" was written in Colombia. But his best poem in this vein—"Night"—was written later (in Solentiname) and thereby missed inclusion in *Oración*. It opens and closes with sections based on St. John of the Cross, which enclose a powerful critique of our society—its big-business incentives, its values as reflected in *New Yorker* ads, its juvenile delinquency, its drop-out philosophies and fears, the bogus mysticism of the drug culture (whose visions "are not the Vision"), and the unceasing threat of nuclear war.

The threatened nuclear holocaust provides the core of "Apocalypse," partly inspired by *Breakthrough to Peace* (1962), which Merton edited, and also by Merton's own essay called "A Letter to Pablo Antonio Cuadra Concerning Giants." The last poem in *Oración,* it is a modern rendering of the Book of Revelation, and its Biblical approach grows out of the sequence of up-dated psalms which immediately preceded it. Each of his *Salmos* is a reflection on the Old Testament psalm of the same number, in which he explores its modern relevance. This exegetical technique began as a devotional exercise. The reading of the psalms takes up the greater part of the canonical Hours (the backbone of communal monastic prayer), and Cardenal found that they became more meaningful if inwardly transposed to fit the circumstances of the modern world, whose joys and terrors all had parallels in those of the Old Testament. Of the two given here, Psalm 150 ("The Cosmos Is His Sanctuary") is a song of praise, crowning a cycle of poems which move beyond the poet's continent to share the worldwide sufferings of twentieth-century man—no longer just in the torture chambers of Nicaragua or Brazil, but in the concentration camps of World War II, in Hiroshima, in isolation hospitals, and in the wards for terminal cases. (The other psalm in this anthology, Psalm 57, is very much later—1972—and it reflects a very different mood, the subject of a later comment.) Not all the *Salmos* are equally successful, but they are the most translated of his works, and the best ones have passed the test of liturgical use in various languages. Nevertheless, the much longer Amerindian poems—chiefly written in Solentiname—have a deeper kind of strength.

Yet the finest of Cardenal's poems, to date, is probably the elegiac "Coplas on the Death of Merton," composed over a period of about a year after Merton had been accidentally electrocuted in Bangkok (December 10, 1968). Although a song of mourning, it is vibrant with rejoicing. The most complex of all Cardenal's poems, it uses almost every technique which he had ever employed, including abrupt Poundian cross-cutting and collage (by now both dominant features of his style). It also handles an immense—sometimes a bewildering—variety of references: religious readings at Gethsemani, the classics, the Chinese poetry he learnt to love through Merton, primitive beliefs about the afterlife, English phrases from the media, advertisements into which he read symbolic meanings, and a wealth of personal reminiscence. Intricately structured, and full of internal echoes, it works in both an elusive and an allusive way—the splicing deftly building up a flow of images which ultimately leaves the reader with a deep sense of abiding peace. Rexroth's version (made in collaboration with Mireya Jaimes-Freyre) is itself a personal tribute, both to Merton and to Cardenal—who had translated Rexroth's own variation on the *Ubi sunt?* motif, "Between Two Wars" ("*¿Recuerdas aquel desayuno de noviembre?*"), many years before.

Merton's death marked the end of an era in Cardenal's life, and the "Coplas" mark the culmination of a period in his poetry. Looking back over his life and thought, and over the poems written since the completion of the "Coplas," the end of the 1960s seems a watershed in his career: something like the termination of a cycle in the Mayan calendar. In more ways than one, it was what "Katún 11 Ahau" had called

> the time for building the new pyramid
> upon the basis of the old.

At the end of each period of cyclic time the Mayan temples were rebuilt, not (as with our structures) after demolition, but by enclosing the older pyramid inside a new one: necessarily larger (though not necessarily better) and exhibiting the features of a later cultural phase.

That poem had used the terminology of the *Chilam Balam* (the Mayan sacred book) to characterize the evils of present-day existence in Latin America, where authoritarian violence has become as institutionalized as exploitation and corruption. Its cyclic title date, which alludes to the arrival of the Spaniards, associates the coming of an old colonialism with present evils (seen, at least by implication, as in part the consequences of an equivalent dependency). But the *chilán* (the priestly soothsayer: "he that is mouth") regards those very evils as portents of a coming change, when "the *katún* of the Cruel Men will pass" and

> The *Katún* of the Tree of Life will be established. . . .
> The *Katún* Union-for-a-Common-Cause,
> the *Katún* of "Good Living Conditions". . . .

Cardenal had also phrased that message in Biblical terms in his version of Psalm 21, which ends: "There will be a banquet set before the poor, and a great feast among our people, the new people that is going to be born."

The values of such a future had indeed been actualized, on a small scale, in the Solentiname commune, where Cardenal is not only a Catholic priest but a prophet, akin to a Mayan *chilán*. The part the *chilán* played in Mayan culture is the role which Cardenal assigns to himself, the modern poet-priest, as both the initiator of social change and the soothsayer delivering "tablets which predict eclipses" (the bearer of ill-tidings to the tyrants of our age). But when Merton died, Cardenal could still not see a way to imbue the power structure of whole countries with the values of his commune. Establishing Latin American republics whose structures are genuinely based on social justice is harder than setting up a commune, or fostering awareness of those values among students and *campesinos*.

Then, in 1970, he spent three months in Cuba, where he kept a comprehensive diary in prose. In this, he emerges as a perceptive—yet a curiously naïve—observer of the Cuban scene. While noting that the system had its faults, the only thing it seemed to him to lack to be a viable replacement for capitalist society was a sound Christian basis. If its drastic changes in the social order—in the here-and-now of life-on-earth—could but be grounded in theological principles which look beyond this world to a timeless reality, then lasting social justice would be achieved. The New People "that is going to be born" would be a people made up of the New Men whom Che Guevara predicated, but the values of their "communism" would coincide with those of the earliest Christians—whose faith and underground existence (like that of many a Latin American group) Cardenal evokes in the brief poem called "In the Half-Light," written shortly before Merton's death.

Cardenal's Cuban experience was, as he told me in Solentiname, almost "a second conversion." It persuaded him that many things he had thought unattainable this century could really be achieved, but only after such a radical change in the social order. His own form of Pauline Christianity has since become progressively more revolutionary: the kind of Nicaragua of which he dreams in "The Arrival" is a socialist state whose features strikingly recall the Cuban model. All this has modified the ideal of strict nonviolence he shared with Merton, because of his recognition that Latin American society is unlikely to be restructured without recourse to arms—yet he is still deeply unhappy about the need for violence, remaining at heart a "man of peace" in the profoundest sense. Psalm 57 reflects these changes in his thought: God is asked to end the *status quo,* the people will take over and deal out justice, and God is an entirely proletarian God. The title of a very recent book of prose and verse by Cardenal (not yet available in English) is *The Sanctity of Revolution,* and it ends with three poems grouped together by the Spanish publisher as "Poems of Christian-Marxist Inspiration." The earliest of these—"Condensations"—is the last text in this collection. Regarding Revolution as Evolution, it is also an almost mystical canticle of love—both human and divine.

Cardenal's socioreligious thinking has a great appeal in Latin America, and its increasing militancy is symptomatic of much that is happening there among practising Christians. It demands our attention (whatever our own views may be) because it is becoming an important factor in both the spiritual and the political life of the Americas—perhaps even in the broader web of changing relationships between the peoples of the Third World and the First. Cardenal's poems help bridge the gap, mediating between peoples and giving us the "feel" of his situation. Poetry can offer insights of a special kind: experiential rather than discursive. Paradoxically, its "modes of indirection" enable it to strike the more directly home.

Saint Catherine's College, Oxford.   R. P.-M.

Apocalypse
and other poems

ERNESTO
CARDENAL

DRAKE IN THE SOUTHERN SEA

I set out from the Port of Acapulco on the twenty-third of March
and kept a steady course until Saturday, the fourth of April, when
a half hour before dawn, we saw by the light of the moon
that a ship had come alongside
with sails and a bow that seemed to be of silver.
Our helmsman cried out to them to stand off
but no one answered, as though they were all asleep.
Again we called out: "Where did their ship come from?"
and they said: "Peru!"
After which we heard trumpets, and muskets firing,
and they ordered me to come down into their longboat
to cross over to where their Captain was.
I found him walking the deck,
went up to him, kissed his hands and he asked me
what silver or gold I had aboard that ship.
I said, "None at all,
none at all, My Lord, only my dishes and cups."
So then he asked me if I knew the Viceroy.
I said I did. And I asked the Captain
if he were Captain Drake himself and no other.
The Captain replied that
he was the very Drake I spoke of.
We spoke together a long time, until the hour of dinner,
and he commanded that I sit by his side.
His dishes and cups are of silver, bordered with gold
with his crest upon them.
He has with him many perfumes and scented waters in crystal vials
which, he said, the Queen had given him.
He dines and sups always with music of violins
and also takes with him everywhere painters who keep painting
all the coast for him.
He is a man of some twenty-four years, small, with a reddish beard.
He is a nephew of Juan Aquinas,[1] the pirate,

[1] John Hawkins.—T. M.

3

and is one of the greatest mariners there are upon the sea.
The day after, which was Sunday, he clothed himself in
      splendid garments
and had them hoist all their flags
with pennants of divers colors at the mastheads,
the bronze rings, and chains, and the railings and
the lights on the Alcazar shining like gold.
His ship was like a gold dragon among the dolphins.
And we went, with his page, to my ship to look at the coffers.
All day long until night he spent looking at what I had.
What he took from me was not much,
a few trifles of my own,
and he gave me a cutlass and a silver brassart for them,
asking me to forgive him
since it was for his lady that he was taking them.
He would let me go, he said, the next morning, as soon as
      there was a breeze.
For this I thanked him, and kissed his hands.
He is carrying, in his galleon, three thousand bars of silver, ·
three coffers full of gold,
twelve great coffers of pieces of eight.
And he says he is heading for China
following the charts and steered by a Chinese pilot whom
      he captured.

[T. M].

Note: This poem is based on a strictly historical account of the en-
counter with Drake written by a Spanish captain, in a letter to the Viceroy
of New Spain, dated Realejo (Nicaragua), 1579.—E. C.

ABOVE THE RAIN-SOAKED TRACK

Above the rain-soaked track down which the girls with their jars
come and go,
      on steps cut in the rock,
from the trees hung great lianas
like heads of hair or snakes.
There was a superstitious feeling in the air.

Below:
       the lemon-hued lagoon,
            like polished jade.
Cries would rise from the water
and the sound of mud-colored bodies plunging into water.
            A superstitious feeling. . . .
The girls came and went, with their jars,
singing an old love-song as they passed.
Those who came up, erect as statues:
beneath their cool red amphoræ with painted patterns,
            cool bodies, with the shape of amphoræ.
And those who went down
       went prancing and dancing, leapt like deer,
their skirts unfolding in the wind like flowers.

                                        [R. P.-M.]

EPIGRAMS

              . . . but you will not escape from my iambs . . .—Catullus

1

I give you these verses, Claudia, because they belong to you.
I've written them plainly so you can understand them.
They're just for you, but if they bore you,
maybe one day they'll spread, all through Spanish America . . .
and if you also scorn the love that wrote them,
other women will dream of this love that was not meant for them.
And perhaps you'll see, Claudia, that these poems
(written to court you) inspire
in other loving couples who read them
the kisses that the poet did not inspire in you.

                                        [D. D. W.]

2

Be careful, Claudia, when you're with me,
because the slightest gesture, any word, a sigh

of Claudia, the slightest slip,
perhaps one day scholars will examine it,
and this dance of Claudia's will be remembered for centuries.
I've warned you, Claudia.

[D. D. W.]

3

Of all these movies, Claudia, of these parties,
of these horse races,
nothing will be left for posterity
except the verses of Ernesto Cardenal to Claudia
    (if even that)
and Claudia's name that I put in those verses
and the names of my rivals, in case I decide to snatch them
from oblivion and to include them also in my verses
to make fun of them.

[D. D. W.]

4

Others maybe'll earn a lot of money
but I've sacrificed that money
to write these songs to you
or to another girl I'll praise instead of you
or to nobody at all.

[D. D. W.]

5

When I lost you we both lost:
I lost because you were what I loved most
and you lost because I was the one who loved you most.
But between the two of us you lose more than I do:
for I can love others the way I loved you
but you'll never be loved the way you were loved by me.

[D. D. W.]

6

You girls who one day will read these verses all stirred up
and will dream about a poet:
know that I wrote them for a girl like you
and it was all in vain.

[D. D. W.]

7

This will be my revenge:
that one day you'll hold in your hands the book of a famous poet
and you'll read these lines that the author wrote for you
and you won't even know it.

[D. D. W.]

8

They told me you were in love with another man
and then I went off to my room
and I wrote that article against the Government
that landed me in jail.

[D. D. W.]

9

She was sold to Kelly & Martínez, Inc.,
and many people will send her silver wedding presents,
and others will send her silver-plated presents,
and her one-time lover sends her this epigram.

[D. D. W.]

10

You who are proud of my verses
not because I wrote them

but because you inspired them
even though they were written against you:

    You might have inspired better poetry.
    You might have inspired better poetry.

[D. D. W.]

11

I've handed out underground leaflets,
shouting Long Live Freedom! in the middle of the street
defying the armed guards.
I took part in the April Rebellion:
but I grow pale when I pass by your house
and one glance from you makes me tremble.

[D. D. W.]

12

Take these Costa Rican roses,
Myriam, with these love verses:
my verses will remind you that rose faces
are like your face; the roses
will remind you that love must be cut off
and that your face will fade like Greece and Rome.
When there is no more love or Costa Rican roses,
you'll remember, Myriam, this sad song.

[D. D. W.]

13   *Imitation of Propertius*

I sing not of the defense of Stalingrad
or of the Egyptian Campaign
or of the landing on Sicily
or of General Eisenhower's crossing of the Rhine:

I sing only of the courting of a girl.

8

Not with the jewels of the Morlock Jewelry Store
nor with Dreyfus Perfumes
nor with orchids inside their plastic box
nor with a Cadillac
but just with my poems I courted her.

And she prefers me, even though I'm poor, to all Somoza's millions.

[D. D. W.]

14

You've worked twenty years
to pile up twenty million *pesos,*
but we'd give twenty million *pesos*
not to have to work the way you've worked.

[D. D. W.]

15

You don't deserve even an epigram.

[D. D. W.]

16

I still remember that street with yellow lamps,
with that full moon between the electric wires,
and that star on the corner, a far-off radio,
the Merced Church tower striking eleven:
and the golden light of your open door, on that street.

[D. D. W.]

17

Our love was born in May with *malinches* in flower—
when the *malinches* are in flower in Managua—.
They flower only in that month: in other months they bear vexations.

But the *malinches* will flower again in May
and the love that's gone won't return again.

[D. D. W.]

18

Suddenly in the night the sirens
sound their long, long, long alarm,
the siren's miserable howl
of fire, or death's white ambulance
like a ghost wailing in the night,
coming closer and closer above the streets
and the houses, it rises, rises, and falls,
and it grows, grows, falls and goes away
growing and dying. It's neither a fire nor a death:
        Just the Dictator flashing by.

[T. M.]

19

Some shots were heard last night.
Out by the burial ground.
No one knows who they killed, or how many.
No one knows a thing.
Some shots were heard last night.
That's all.

[T. M.]

20

You are alone among the crowds
as the moon is alone
and the sun is alone in the sky.

Yesterday you were in the stadium
in the midst of thousands of people
and I spotted you as soon as I entered

just as if you'd been alone
in an empty stadium.

[D. D. W.]

21

If you are in New York
in New York there's nobody else
and if you're not in New York
in New York there's nobody.

[D. D. W.]

22

But in the night you see your rice and your fried beans,
with a fresh cheese and a hot tortilla,
or a roast banana,
                you eat them without a bodyguard.
And your pitcher of cocoa is not first tasted by an adjutant.
And afterwards, if you want to, you can play a country song on
        your guitar,
and you don't sleep surrounded by floodlights and barbed wire
        and watchtowers.

[D .D. W.]

23

Your eyes are a moon shimmering on a black lagoon
and your hair the black waves beneath the moonless sky
and the owl flying in the black night.

[D. D. W.]

24

Yesterday I saw you on the street, Myriam, and
you looked so lovely to me, Myriam, that
(how can I explain to you how lovely you looked!)

not even you, Myriam, can see yourself so lovely or
imagine you can look so lovely to me.
And you looked so lovely that it seems to me that
no woman is lovelier than you
nor does any lover see any woman
so lovely, Myriam, as I see you
and even you, Myriam, can hardly be so lovely
(because so much loveliness can not be real!)
as the way I saw you yesterday so lovely on the street,
and as it seems to me today, Myriam, that I saw you.

[D. D. W.]

25

Recall the many lovely girls that have existed:
all the beauties of Troy, and those of Achæa
and those of Thebes, and of the Rome of Propertius.
And many of them let love pass by,
and they died, and they've been dead for centuries.
You who are lovely now on the streets of Managua,
like them one day you'll belong to a distant past,
when the gas stations will be romantic ruins.

Remember the beauties of the streets of Troy!

[D. D. W.]

26

Ah, you, pitiless one,
        crueler than young Tacho.

[D. D. W.]

27

There is a place next to the Tiscapa Lagoon—
a bench under a *quelite* tree—
that you know (the girl I'm writing
these verses for will know they're for her).

And you remember that bench and that *quelite;*
the moon reflected in the Tiscapa Lagoon,
the lights of the dictator's palace,
the frogs croaking down there in the lagoon.
That *quelite* tree is still there;
the same lights still shine;
the moon is reflected in the Tiscapa Lagoon;
but tonight that bench will be empty,
or it will have another couple, not us.

[D. D. W.]

28

My sweet kitten, my sweet kitten!
How my sweet kitten trembles
as I stroke her face and neck
and as you murder and torture!

[D. D. W.]

29

In Costa Rica the teamsters sing.
They travel the roads with mandolins.
And the carts go by painted like parrots,
and the oxen move with colored ribbons
and little bells and flowers on their horns.

When it's coffee picking time in Costa Rica
and the carts go by loaded with coffee.

And there are bands in the town squares,
and in San José the balconies and windows
are filled with girls and flowers.
And the girls stroll around the park.
And the President can walk the streets in San José.

[D. D. W.]

They killed you and they wouldn't tell us where they buried
        your body,
but ever since the whole country has been your tomb;
or rather: in every inch of the country where your body does
        not lie, you have risen from the dead.

They thought they were killing you with an order to fire.
They thought they were burying you
and what they were doing was burying a seed.

[D. D. W.]

31   *Somoza Unveils Somoza's Statue of Somoza in the
        Somoza Stadium*

It's not that I think the people raised this statue to me,
because I know better than you do that I ordered it myself.
Nor that I have any illusions about passing with it into posterity
because I know the people one day will tear it down.
Nor that I wished to erect to myself in life
the monument you'll not erect to me in death:
I put up this statue just because I know you'll hate it.

[D. D. W.]

32

Every evening she'd walk with her mother along
        the Landestrasse
and at the corner of the Schmiedtor, every evening,
there was Hitler waiting for her, to watch her go by.
The taxis and the buses were filled with kisses
and the couples rented boats on the Danube.
But he didn't know how to dance. He never dared to speak to her.
Later she'd go by without her mother, with a cadet.
And still later she didn't go by at all.

That's why we had the Gestapo, the annexation of Austria, the World War.

[D. D. W.]

33 *Epitaph for Joaquín Pasos*

Here he walked, through these streets, unemployed, jobless,
and without a nickel.
Only poets, whores, and drunkards knew his verses.
He never went abroad.
He was in prison.
Now he's dead.
He has no monument.
                    But
remember him when you have concrete bridges,
great turbines, tractors, silver-colored granaries,
good governments.
Because in his poems he purified his people's language
which one day will be used to write the commercial treaties,
the Constitution, the love letters, and the decrees.

[D. D. W.]

34

The National Guard is out searching for a man.
A man is hoping tonight to reach the frontier.
The name of that man is not known.
There are many more men buried in a trench.
The numbers and the names of those men are not known.
Nor are the location and the number of the trenches known.
The National Guard is out searching for a man.
A man is hoping tonight to escape from Nicaragua.

[D. D. W.]

35

Our poems can't be published yet.
They circulate from hand to hand, in manuscript

or mimeograph. But one day
people will forget the name of the dictator
against whom they were written,
but they'll go on reading them.

[D. D. W.]

36

Maybe we'll get married this year,
my love, and we'll have a little house.
And maybe my book'll get published,
or we'll both go abroad.
Maybe Somoza will fall, my love.

[D. D. W.]

37   *A Girl's Song*

My long hair! My long hair!
You wanted your girl to have long hair.
Now I have it down below my shoulders
and you didn't wait for my long hair.

[D. D. W.]

38

Do you think this corner with the woman selling guavas
where you met me with terror and with joy
(even if you showed only pallor and silence)
will be wiped out by Los Angeles and the Champs-Elysées?

[D. D. W.]

39   *Corn-Island*

The water of South West Bay is bluer than the sky
but your eyes are bluer than South West Bay

and in Brig Bay Cave there is a pirate treasure
but your curls are worth more than the treasure of Brig Bay.

[D. D. W.]

40

Now the May rains have come,
the scarlet *malinches* have blossomed again
and Diriá Road is joyful, full of puddles:
                but now you are not with me.

[D. D. W.]

41

Haven't you read, my love, in the *News:*
SENTINEL OF PEACE, GENIUS OF WORK
PALADIN OF DEMOCRACY IN AMERICA
DEFENDER OF CATHOLICISM IN AMERICA
THE PROTECTOR OF THE PEOPLE
                THE BENEFACTOR . . . ?
They plunder the people's language.
And they falsify the people's words.
(Just like the people's money.)
That's why we poets do so much polishing on a poem.
And that's why my love poems are important.

[D. D. W.]

42

We wake up with guns going off
and the dawn alive with planes—
It sounds like a revolution:
it's only the Tyrant's birthday.

[T. M.]

Ileana: the Galaxy of Andromeda,
at 700,000 light years,
that the naked eye can see on a clear night,
is closer than you.
Other solitary eyes will be looking at me from Andromeda,
in their night. You I do not see.
Ileana: distance is time, and time flies.
At 200 million miles an hour the universe
is expanding toward nothingness.
And you are like millions of years away from me.

[D. D. W.]

44

As the jackiedaw sings at night
to the jackdaw on another branch:
    "Jackdaw,
  if you want me to go, I'll go,
  if you want me to go, I'll go,"
and the jackdaw calls her to his branch:
    "Jackiedaw,
  if you want to come, come,
  if you want to come, come,"
and when she goes off to where he is
the jackdaw goes off to another branch:
  so I call to you
        and you go off.
  So I call to you
        and off you go.

[D. D. W.]

45

If at the time of the April revolt
I'd been killed with the rest
I wouldn't have known you:

and if the April revolt had come now
I'd have been killed with the rest.

[D. D. W.]

46

When the golden asters blossomed
we were both in love.
The asters still have blossoms
and now we're a couple of strangers.

[D. D. W.]

47

The heavy drops are like
footsteps climbing the stairs
and the wind beating against the door
like a woman about to come in.

[D. D. W.]

48

You came to visit me in dreams
but the emptiness you left behind when you went away
was real.

[D. D. W.]

49

The person closest to me
is you, and yet
I haven't seen you for ages
except in dreams.

[D. D. W.]

Have you heard in the night the cry of the anteater
      oo-oo-oo-oo
or the coyote in the moonlit night
      uuuuuuuuuuuuuuuuuuu?
Well, that's just what these verses are.

                [D. D. W.]

NNW

When fox cubs are born and tadpoles hatch
and the male butterfly dances in front of the female
and the kingfishers touch beaks
and the light grows longer and ovaries swell,
the swallows will return from the South. . . .
Will "return" from the South?
                      "The dark swallows"
those that flew off in September to North Africa,
crowded every curving loop of wire,
darkened the afternoons,
and filled the sky with voices,
those will not return.

And the eels that swam downriver in Africa
and sought the Sargasso Sea to consummate
their nuptials clad in silver wedding garments,
like the ladies of the Court of King Don Juan:
where are they now?
                The *palolos* of the Southern Seas
which rise to the surface at their feast of fecundation
when the November moon is at its full
and cover the whole sea those nights with phosphorescent foam
and sink back beneath the sea not to return?

And the gilded *catopsilias* garbed like Queen Thi
that migrate each autumn NNW
leaving behind the nectar, flowers, the mating

with nothing ahead save billows, salt, sea-loneliness
and death (lying NNW)
　　　　North-North-West
but on a steady bearing NNW?

　　　　　　　　　[R. P.-M.]

THERE IS A HUM OF TRACTORS

There is a hum of tractors in the fields.
The cherry trees are pink with blossom.
And, look, the apple trees are in full bloom.
This, Beloved, is the season of love.
The starlings sing in the sycamore.
The roads smell of fresh tar
and passing cars bear laughing girls.
Look: the season of love has come.
Each bird that flies has one pursuing it.

　　　　　　　　　[R. P.-M.]

A JET IN THE EVENING SKY

A jet in the evening sky,
vapor like a thread,
as the sun sets, golden.
The plane too fast to see:
the golden flight lingers.

　　　　　　　[R. P.-M.]

LIKE EMPTY BEER CANS

Like empty beer cans, like empty
　　cigarette butts;

my days have been like that.
Like figures passing on a
    T.V. screen.
And disappearing, so my
    life has gone.
Like cars going by fast
    on the roads
with girls laughing and radios
    playing . . .
Beauty got obsolete as fast
    as car models
and forgotten radio hits.
Nothing is left of those
    days, nothing,
but empty beer cans,
    cigarette butts,
smiles on faded photos, torn
    tickets
and the sawdust with which,
    in the mornings,
they swept out the bars.

[T. M.]

I DO NOT KNOW

I do not know who is out in the snow.
All that is seen in the snow is his white habit
and at first I saw no one at all:
only the plain white sunlit snow.
The novice in the snow is barely visible.
And I feel that there is something more in this snow
which is neither snow nor novice, and is not seen.

[T. M.]

THIS AUTO HORN

This auto horn sounds familiar.
So does this wind in the pines.
This rattling zinc noviciate roof
reminds me of my house at home.
They are calling to me from the auto.
But my house, near the road
where the cars went by all day
was sold years ago and strangers live in it.
This was no known car. It is gone.
The wind is the same. Only the sighing
of this rainy autumn evening is well known.

[T. M.]

THE MARMOTS IN THEIR BURROWS

The marmots in their burrows are not dead,
they sleep. Nor are the chipmunks dead,
nor have they gone away: curled up,
they lie asleep beneath the earth.
Adders sleep beneath dead leaves;
frogs, buried deep in frozen mud
down by the icebound river, also sleep.
The river sleeps as well. Life is asleep.
In caves, cracks, hollows, secret galleries,
eggs, silk cocoons, seeds, buds
all wait for spring. There are tracks in the snow:
the tracks of fox and skunk, each going out
by night, already searching for a mate.
There is a smell of skunk, these nights.

[R. P.-M.]

BEHIND THE MONASTERY

Behind the monastery, down by the road,
there is a cemetery of worn-out things
where lie smashed china, rusty metal,
cracked pipes and twisted bits of wire,
empty cigarette packs, sawdust,
corrugated iron, old plastic, tires beyond repair:
all waiting for the Resurrection, like ourselves.

[R. P.-M.]

THE LOST CITIES

At night, owls fly among the stelæ,
the wildcat snarls along the terraces,
the jaguar roars in towers,
a stray coyote howls in the Great Square
at the image of the moon in the lagoons
which in remote *katúns* were fish ponds.

Now, the animals are real
which in the frescoes were once stylized;
and princes now sell earthen jars in markets.
But how can one inscribe the hieroglyph again?
Again paint jaguars, and dethrone tyrants?
Rebuild again our tropical acropolis,
our rural capitals amid the *milpa* fields?

The jungle thickets full of monuments.
Altars in *milpas*. Arches
with bas-reliefs among the buttressed roots.
In jungle where it seems man never entered,
where only the anteater and the tapir
and the *quetzal* (still garbed like a Maya) go,
there lies an entire city.
When priests went up the Temple of the Jaguar
with jaguar capes, fans of *quetzal* feathers,

deerskin sandals and ritual masks,
shouting went up from the Ball Courts
with drumbeats, and the scent of copal incense
from the sacred chambers of *zapote* wood,
and the smoke of pinewood torches. . . . While underneath Tikal
there is another city a millennium older.
Today the monkeys howl on the *zapote* trees.

There are no names of generals on the stelæ.

In their temples and palaces and pyramids
and in their calendars and chronicles and codices
there is not one name of a leader or chief or emperor
or priest or politician or commander or governor;
nor did they record political events on monuments,
nor administrations, nor dynasties,
nor ruling families, nor political parties.
In centuries, not one glyph recording a man's name:
the archaeologists still do not know how they were governed.

Their language had no word for "master."
Nor a word for "city wall." They did not wall their cities.
Their cities were cities of temples, they lived in the fields,
among the palm groves and the *milpas* and the pawpaw trees.
Their temple arch was modeled on their hut.
Highways were only for processions.
Religion was the only bond between them,
but it was a religion freely accepted,
imposing no burden. No oppression.
Their priests had no temporal power
and the pyramids were built without forced labor.
At its height their civilization did not turn into an empire.
Nor had they colonies. Nor did they know the arrow.

They knew Jesus as the God of the Maize
and gave him simple offerings
of maize, of birds, of feathers.
They had no wars, nor knew the wheel,
but they had calculated the synodic path of Venus:
every night they noted the rising of Venus
on the horizon, over some distant *ceiba* tree,

as pairs of parrots flew homing to their nests.
They had no metallurgy. Their tools were of stone,
they never left the Stone Age, technologically speaking.
But they computed precise dates going back
four hundred million years.
They had no applied sciences. They were not practical.
Their progress lay in religion, mathematics, art,
astronomy. They had no means of weighing.
They adored time: the mysterious
effluxion of time.
Time was holy. Days were gods.
The past and the future are intermingled in their songs.
They used the same *katúns* for past and future,
in the belief that time was re-enacted
like the motions of the heavenly bodies they observed.
Yet the time which they adored abruptly ceased.
Stelæ remained unfinished,
blocks half cut in quarries
where they still lie.

Only lonely gum-tappers traverse the Petén today.
Vampire bats nest in the stucco friezes.
Wild pigs grunt in the avenues at nightfall.
The jaguar roars in towers—towers root-entangled—
far away in a distant square a lone coyote bays the moon,
and the Pan American jet flies high above the pyramid.
But will the past *katúns* one day return?

[R. P.-M.]

THE VALE OF CUERNAVACA
FROM THE MONASTERY

When there's been rain,
the air above the Vale is even clearer:
            the smoke of huts yet whiter
                        the volcanoes a deeper blue
        the bells yet more distinct.

26

A barefoot lad
drives cattle
down the stony track.

On the blue mountains, even bluer shadows:
          shadows of contours
or perhaps of clouds.
               (And a single small red bird
                    on the telephone wire.)

The smoke of the huts rises
among the corn: and that of the brick kiln.
There is a factory a long way off, at the very
foot of the hills, whose smoke is far far higher.
                    And on the bluish plateau
the long smoke of a train, and its long whistle.

The sound of cars accelerating,
and buses, down on the main road.
               And the tap tap of the stonebreaker
               hammering away at his stones.
On this side: a heavy truck
                    grinding up a hill. . . .

Goats pass with tinkling bells,
leave lingering on the air
a gentle smell of goat
and goat's milk.
               The birds are singing;
in Santa María de Ahuacatitlán
bells are ringing.

The setting sun gilds Teposteco
and tinges the snow on Popo pink.
               Cone
like strawberry ice-cream.

The moon comes up behind
Popocatépetl.

          •   •   •

(A moon tenuous as a cloud
and a cloud above Popo like snow
with Popo's snow the moon.)

.   .   .

The lights of Cuernavaca twinkle in the distance:
those of Cuautla too, farther, almost in the sky,
tiny and bunched together, almost among the stars.
Somewhere in the fields a radio, playing a *corrido*.
A million crickets chirping in the pastures.
        Each chirps and stops and chirps.
Do crickets never sleep?
             And fireflies
flicker like stars, like Cuautla,
like Cuernavaca.

.   .   .

A train whistles in the distance,
deep in the night.
        Mournfully,
three times.
The old train to the capital,
like a lonely bird
calling its missing mate.

        [R. P-M.]

ON LAKE NICARAGUA

Slow cargo-launch, midnight, mid-lake,
bound from San Miguelito to Granada.
The lights ahead not yet in sight,
the dwindling ones behind completely gone.
Only the stars
(the mast a finger pointing to the Seven Sisters)
        and the moon, rising above Chontales.

Another launch (just one red light) goes by
and sinks into the night.
We, for them:
        another red light sinking in the night. . . .

And I, watching the stars, lying on the deck
between bunches of bananas and Chontales cheeses,
wonder: perhaps there's one that is an earth like ours
and someone's watching me (watching the stars)
from another launch, on another night, on another lake.

[R. P.-M.]

MANAGUA 6:30 P.M.

The neon lights are gentle in the twilight
and the mercury lamps are pale and beautiful. . . .
And the red star of a radio tower
is as lovely as Venus
in Managua in the evening sky
and an Esso advertisement is like the moon

There is something mystical about the red tail-lights of cars

(The soul is like a girl kiss-smothered behind a car)
        TACA BUNGE KLM SINGER
        MENNEN HTM GÓMEZ NORGE
        RPM SAF ÓPTICA SELECTA
proclaim the glory of God!
(Kiss me beneath the neon signs oh Lord)
        KODAK TROPICAL RADIO F&C REYES
spell out Your Name
in many-colored lights.
                    "They bear
the good tidings . . ."
I recognize no other
meaning in them
I do not defend the cruelties behind these lights
And if I am to give a verdict on my age
it is this: Barbarous and primitive it was
but yet poetic

        [R. P.-M.]

UNRIGHTEOUS MAMMON (LUKE 16:9)

In respect of riches, then, just or unjust,
of goods be they ill-gotten or well-gotten:
All riches are unjust.
All goods,
　　　　ill-gotten.
If not by you, by others.
Your title deeds may be in order. But
did you buy your land from its true owner?
And he from its true owner? And the latter . . . ?
Though your title go back to the grant of a king
was
the land ever the king's?
Has no one ever been deprived of it?
And the money you receive legitimately now
from client or Bank or National Funds
　　　　　or from the U.S. Treasury,
was it ill-gotten at no point? Yet
do not think that in the Perfect Communist State
Christ's parables will have lost relevance
Or Luke 16:9 have lost validity
　　　　　and riches be no longer UNJUST
or that you will no longer have a duty to distribute riches!

[R. P.-M.]

PRAYER FOR MARILYN MONROE

Lord
accept this girl called Marilyn Monroe throughout the world
though that was not her name
(but You know her real name, that of the orphan raped at nine,
the shopgirl who tried to kill herself aged just sixteen)
who now goes into Your presence without make-up
without her Press Agent
without her photographs or signing autographs
lonely as an astronaut facing the darkness of outer space.

When she was a child, she dreamed she was naked in a church
                    (according to *Time*)
standing in front of a prostrate multitude, heads to the ground,
and had to walk on tiptoe to avoid the heads.
You know our dreams better than the psychiatrists.
Church, house, or cave all represent the safety of the womb
but also something more. . . .
The heads are admirers, so much is clear (that
mass of heads in the darkness below the beam to the screen).
But the temple isn't the studio of 20th-Century Fox.
The temple, of gold and marble, is the temple of her body
in which the Son of Man stands whip in hand
driving out the money-changers of 20th-Century Fox
who made Your house of prayer a den of thieves.

Lord,
in this world defiled by radioactivity and sin,
surely You will not blame a shopgirl
who (like any other shopgirl) dreamed of being a star.
And her dream became "reality" (Technicolor reality).
All she did was follow the script we gave her,
that of our own lives, but it was meaningless.
Forgive her Lord and forgive all of us
for this our 20th Century
and the Mammoth Super-Production in whose making we all shared.

She was hungry for love and we offered her tranquilizers.
For the sadness of our not being saints
                    they recommended Psychoanalysis.
Remember Lord her increasing terror of the camera
and hatred of make-up (yet her insistence on fresh make-up
for each scene) and how the terror grew
and how her unpunctuality at the studios grew.

Like any other shopgirl
she dreamed of being a star.
And her life was as unreal as a dream an analyst reads and files.

Her romances were kisses with closed eyes
which when the eyes are opened
are seen to have been played out beneath the spotlights
                    and the spotlights are switched off

and the two walls of the room (it was a set) are taken down
while the Director moves away notebook in hand,
   the scene being safely canned.
Or like a cruise on a yacht, a kiss in Singapore, a dancc in Rio,
a reception in the mansion of the Duke and Duchess of Windsor
    viewed in the sad tawdriness of a cheap apartment.

The film ended without the final kiss.
They found her dead in bed, hand on the phone.
And the detectives never learned who she was going to call.
It was as
though someone had dialed the only friendly voice
and heard a prerecorded tape just saying "WRONG NUMBER";
or like someone wounded by gangsters, who
reaches out toward a disconnected phone.

Lord, whoever
it may have been that she was going to call
but did not (and perhaps it was no one at all
or Someone not in the Los Angeles telephone book),
   Lord, You pick up that phone.

      [R. P.-M.]

THE COSMOS IS HIS SANCTUARY (PSALM 150)

Praise the Lord in the cosmos
      His sanctuary
with a radius of a hundred thousand million light years
Praise Him through the stars
      and the interstellar spaces
Praise Him through the galaxies
       and the intergalactic spaces
Praise Him through the atoms
      and the interatomic voids
Praise Him with the violin and the flute
       and with the saxophone

Praise Him with the clarinets and with the horn
    with bugles and trombones
                        with cornets and trumpets
Praise Him with violas and cellos
                    with pianos and pianolas
Praise Him with blues and jazz
                 and with symphonic orchestras
with Negro spirituals
              and with Beethoven's Fifth
    with guitars and marimbas
Praise Him with record players
               and with magnetic tapes
Let everything that breathes praise the Lord
    every living cell
              Hallelujah

               [D. D. W.]

APOCALYPSE

AND BEHOLD
I saw an Angel
            (all his cells were electronic eyes)
and I heard a supersonic voice
saying: Open up thy typewriter and type
       and I beheld a silver projectile in flight
    which went from Europe to America in twenty minutes
and the name of the projectile was the H-Bomb
                  (and hell flew with it)
        and I saw a kind of flying saucer fall from heaven
And the seismographs platted a shock like an earthquake
and all the artificial planets fell to earth
    and the President of the National Radiation Council
    the Director of the Atomic Energy Commission
    the Secretary of Defense
         were all deep in their sheltering caves
and the first Angel set off the warning siren
    and from the heavens rained Strontium 90
              Caesium 137
              Carbon 14

and the second Angel set off the warning siren
and all eardrums for 300 miles were shattered
by the sound of the explosion
all retinas which saw the flash of the explosion
were seared throughout those same 300 miles
                    the heat at ground zero was like that of the sun
and steel and iron and glass and concrete were burnt up
                        and sucked into the skies to fall as radioactive rain
and there was loosed a hurricane wind the force of Hurricane Flora
and three million cars and trucks flew up into the skies
and crashed into buildings bursting
                                    like Molotov cocktails
and the third Angel set off the warning siren
and I beheld a mushroom cloud above New York
                            and a mushroom cloud above Moscow
        and a mushroom cloud above London
                            and a mushroom cloud above Peking
(and Hiroshima's fate was envied)
And all the stores and all the museums and all the libraries
and all the beauties of the earth
                            were turned to vapor
and went to form part of the cloud of radioactive dust
which hung above the planet poisoning it
        the radioactive rain gave leukemia unto some
                                lung cancer unto others
            and unto others cancer of the bone
                                    or cancer of the ovaries
children were born with cataracts
and the genes of man suffered unto the twenty-second generation.
                        And this was known as the 45-Minute War. . . .
        Seven Angels came
bearing cups of smoke in their hands
                    (smoke like a mushroom cloud)
and first I saw the great cup raised over Hiroshima
                        (like a cone of venomous ice cream)
                engendering one vast malignant ulcer
and the cup of the second was poured into the sea
        making the whole sea radioactive
                                    so that all the fishes died
and the third Angel poured forth a neutronic cup

and it was given unto him to sear men with a fire like solar fire
and the fourth Angel poured his cup which was of Cobalt
and it was given unto Babylon to drain the chalice of the grapes
                                                        of wrath
And the loud voice cried:
                Smite her with twice the megatons with which she smote!
And the Angel who controlled the firing of this bomb
                                        pushed down the firing key
And they said unto me: Thou hast as yet not seen the Typhus Bomb
                    nor yet Q Fever
I continued watching the vision in the night
and in my vision I beheld as on TV
emerging from the masses
                a Machine
        fearful and terrible beyond all measure
and like a bear or an eagle or a lion with the wings of aircraft
many propellers numerous antennae eyes of radar
its brain a computer programmed to give the Number of the Beast
roaring through hosts of microphones
                                        and it gave orders unto men
and all men went in fear of the Machine
Likewise I saw the aircraft in my vision
aircraft faster than sound bearing 50-megaton bombs
and no man guided them but the Machine alone
and they flew toward every city of the earth
each one precisely on target
And the Angel said: Canst thou see where Columbus Circle was?
                Or the place where the United Nations Building stood?
And where Columbus Circle was
                I saw a hole which could contain a 50-story building
and where the United Nations Building stood
I saw only a great gray cliff covered with moss and duck shit
with wave-swept rocks beyond it and sea gulls crying
And in the heavens I beheld a mighty light
                like a million-megaton explosion
and I heard a voice saying unto me: Switch on thy radio
and I did switch it on and heard: BABYLON IS FALLEN
                        BABYLON THE GREAT IS
                                                FALLEN
and all transmitters in the world gave the same news

35

And the Angel gave me a check drawn on the National City Bank
and said unto me: Go thou cash this check
but no bank would for all the banks were bankrupt
Skyscrapers were as though they had never been
A million simultaneous fires yet not one firefighter
nor a phone to summon an ambulance nor were there any ambulances
nor was there enough plasma in all the world
                                        to help the injured of a single city
And I heard another voice from heaven saying:
                                        Go forth from her my people
Lest ye be contaminated by the Radiation
                        lest ye be smitten by the Microbes
        by the Anthrax Bomb
                        by the Cholera Bomb
                by the Diphtheria Bomb
                                by the Tularemia Bomb
They will behold the great disaster on TV
                                for the Bomb is fallen on great Babylon
and they will weep and wail for the Beloved City
pilots will look down from their planes afraid to approach
the ocean liners will stay anchored far away
for fear lest the atomic leprosy should fall on them
On every waveband there was a voice heard saying:
                ALLELUIA
And the Angel carried me away into the wilderness
                        and the wilderness blossomed with laboratories
and there the Devil carried out his atomic tests
and I beheld the Great Whore riding on the Beast
(the Beast was a technological Beast all slogan-bedecked)
and the Whore came clutching all manner of checks and bonds
and shares and commercial documents
her harlot's voice sang drunkenly as in a night club
in her left hand she bore a cup of blood
and she was drunk with the blood of all those tortured
all those purged all those condemned by military courts
all those sent to the wall
and of whoever had resisted upon earth
                                with all the martyrs of Jesus
and she laughed with her gold teeth
                        the lipstick on her lips was blood

and the Angel said unto me: the heads which thou dost see on
    the Beast are dictators,
and their horns are revolutionary leaders who are not dictators yet
but they will be later
and these shall make war against the Lamb
                      and the Lamb shall overcome them
And he said unto me: The nations of the world are split into 2 blocks
            (Gog and Magog)
yet the 2 blocks are in truth but the one
(which is against the Lamb)
          and fire will fall from heaven to consume them both
And in the Earth's biology I saw a new Evolution
It was as though a New Planet had appeared in space
For death and hell were cast into the sea of nuclear fire
and neither were there peoples as before
but I saw rather a new species freshly evolved
a species not made up of individuals
but rather one sole organism
                  made up of men in place of cells
and all biologists were mightily amazed
But men were free and in their union were one Person—
            not a Machine—
and the sociologists were equally astounded
Such men as had no part in this new species
           were but as fossils
The Organism enclosed the whole roundness of the planet
round as a cell (but planetary in dimensions)
and the Cell was garlanded as a Bride awaiting the Bridegroom
and the Earth rejoiced
      (as when, dividing, the first cell was wedded)
And there was a New Canticle
and all other inhabited planets heard the Earth singing
    and it was a love-song

[R. P.-M.]

KATÚN 11 AHAU

Katún of dishonorable governors and many arrows,
of sadness in the huts,
                              and whispering,
        and vigilance by night.
In this *katún*
we weep for the books that were burned,
the exiles from the kingdom. The loss
of corn
and of our cosmic knowledge.

Greed and pestilence and rocks and skulls.

Lord Mountain Cat. Lord Honey Bear. The jaguar of the people.
In this *katún* the *chilán* writes:
                              "the people eat stones
                              eat sticks."
The *katún* in which great tributes are collected,
        in which the mask is stolen,
in which the treasure buried in the *milpa* is stolen.
In this *katún* invaders never lack;
                        the enemies of the land.
Suckers of blood . . .
                        Gnats battening on the peoples.
The emptiers of the great earthen jars.
Our life like badgers, in the jungle, is hard.
They scorn our knowledge of the universe:
a book in which we read for people's good.
        (In this *katún* we are derided for our dress.)
                        The hieroglyphs are lost beneath the thickets.
Our Civilization with black vultures overhead.
Our dwellings flattened by the hurricane.
The Nobles now *peones* mending roads.
The people bowed down lugging a mountain in a net.
And governments: they are like the drought. . . .
And we say: would that there might return
                he who first built an arch,
        wrote prayers,
devised the calendar permitting chronicles and histories
                and auguries of things to come.

Now however, in the meanwhile, like badgers.
Saddest of moons,
saddest of moons in the sky of the Petén.
Oppression. . . .
           And vigilance in the night.
Our lord the Honey Bear is lecherous. . . .

The *chilán* ("he that is mouth") writes thus:
       "The Plague is great, and great the Hurricane"
   In the blue sea the pointed fin
   the pointed fin
         of evil-minded Xooc, man-eating shark.

But the *katún* of the Cruel Men will pass.
The Katún of the Tree of Life shall be established.
And a benevolent rule.
The people be no longer bidden to eat less.
The Katún Union-for-a-Common-Cause,
the Katún of "Good living conditions". . . .
No longer shall we have to keep our voices low.
The *chilán* says the people will be a united people.
Many will come together to sing together.
     And then there will be no more Honey Bear.
The stone beneath the thickets will once more have a noble face.
The square stone
        wear a countenance.

The governors will be good, to the people's joy.
   The Lords: legitimate.
Abundance in the mountains, and fair rituals.

It is the time for building the new pyramid
              upon the basis of the old.

The evil-minded Xooc, the Shark, has been harpooned.

And the people will never lack for a *chilán*.
The Chilán:
      he who reads the sacred scriptures
and studies the skies by night.
The movements of the Sun and of the Moon

in order that the time to till the land be known,
the time to harvest corn,

                    to burn the fields,

    to set the traps,
to search the woods for deer.
The Chilán: He sets the days for rain.
The days when men shall sing.
The ending of the rainy season.
Wards off both plagues and hunger.
Distributes food when hunger comes.
Invigilates the carving of the stelæ,

      designs new temples,
delivers tablets which predict eclipses.

                     [R. P.-M.]

NIGHT ·

      The dark night of the soul (or Nothing!)
      Night without moon or sometimes moonlit.
      In the interior emptiness, company.
      An emptiness of all to possess ALL.
      The dark night of kisses: light
      is seen as a cloud in this night.
      In dream and forgetfulness, knowing not how.
      The flavor of love unknowing uncomprehending.
      Night. The supper that rests and that enamors.

And you, what do you want? A share of Du Pont?
To go to bed with Miss Sweden or Miss Brazil?

Fiery Ford 66: luxurious comfort
Ford Galaxy 500/XL flame-colored
in the background city lights in the night
and He and She reclining languorous inside
      He in tuxedo She with an orchid
(impressively new lines . . . daring and elegant
      VISIT YOUR FORD AGENT)

or the yellow Pontiac in green pastures
              with the eternal picnic spread by its side
and She on the deck of the yacht in a check blouse
        dark glasses and a smile full of sunshine
hair gently wind-lifted and the sea blue-green
But do you know that She doesn't exist? She doesn't exist.
Publicity
              is a painted whore!
Or the Pan American Jet Clipper white as snow
              floating in blue blue sky
Royal castle (Kodachrome) in the Bavarian Alps
or palm trees in the foreground and a Tahiti beach
              the place that you saw in your dreams
              and that you thought you'd never reach?
        CONSULT YOUR TRAVEL AGENT
or a walk along a California shore
He and She happy beside the sea
and carrying the picnic basket between them.
A painted whore! No, She doesn't exist!

A share of Du Pont? Or a Du Pont directorship?
Your house with fourteen gardens and Du Pont fungicide
        a twenty-room apartment full of antiques
              (a Georgian mansion?)
Vacations in Honolulu. The Riviera.
Hobbies: salmon fishing in Scotland
                     safaris in Africa
cups won by horse or hound.
Your Du Pont invented Nylon
and before that Cellophane
but earlier still he "made it" by selling gunpowder
(40% of the powder used by the Allies in World War I)
Supersonic planes flying overhead all the time
bomb-laden
                     machines talking to other machines
        kennels with air conditioning
the President assassinated on your TV screen
              babes burned with napalm.
And faces rigid on the subway, rigid
with terror in the offices

the daily terror on the radio
                              and on television.
A bomb in Algeria.
Sometimes in the night, in the depth of our souls,
although we'd not admit it, we've seen Dracula.
            "Incompatibility of character"
        incompatibility for love
and advertisements singing the praises of woman.
And the turning and turning in our sleep each night
those supersonic planes
        flying great circles in the night sky Superman
the bombs are not intended to be used they say

and you buy the product you are meant to buy
and think the thoughts which you are meant to think
dutifully answer all the questionnaires
and heed what the records say
the radio voice which gives you orders.
Shall we rebel? Shall
we smash
                windows? throw bricks at shopfronts?
And would that make us free?
                        Do we free ourselves through Revolution
like juvenile delinquents in stolen cars
careering down roads between billboards?
(They believe every ad they see, they believe
                in trade-names and adore new cars)

Better to be beat saints
        zen cool jazz beards and sandals
always thumbing a lift to some New City
with no firm creed on which to lay their heads
those who pick up trash and shovel snow—
                        Voluntary Poverty.
Poor in the lap of prosperity.
Begging for alms on Insurgentes Avenue with a guitar
or selling a pint of blood to buy a meal
            they read not papers neither do they view TV
nor do they join political parties
Herod and the little foxes have their lairs
but there is nowhere for the Son of Man to lay his head.

They dropped out of civilization. Yet there's
still fear in their eyes. (The air
of someone, in a station, who jumped out
of an express train to an unknown destination)

But their trappings
are really more of a question
                                        a question to others
than an answer
And the visions of lysergic acid
                            are not the Vision
but
fantastic neon visions—
                            from a drugstore—
    Or like the invention of yet another plastic.
Visions sold by gangsters or else sold by Du Pont.
And they are so lonely, so un-united in their night
the night of an expanding universe
like someone who puts an ad in the paper
    "I wish to have correspondence with a young lady 18 to 23
            Box Number . . ."
Or: "I wish to have correspondence with a gentleman . . ."
Or someone asking a computer for a pen-pal
speaking the same language and sharing the same tastes.

And if they have thought they kissed the Infinite
those kisses were lit by General Electric's fluorescent light.

Sor Josefa del Castillo y Guevara: seeker of Nothingness.
Or as Fernando González said to Gonzalo Arango:
Take up thy Cross.
And:
        "If they renounce the world, their world,
                    but achieve not detachment from it . . ."

        The dark night of the soul, or NOTHING.
        An as it were being in the dark with nothing.
        Dark night of kisses. The Lover and the Belovèd.
        Light as a darkness in this night. And Nothing.
        The silent music is not played on nylon strings.

                                        [R. P.-M.]

IN THE HALF-LIGHT

In the half-light
    (the gathering being clandestine)
smiling girls move from table to table
with olives and sardines
        Irene serves the wine
there aren't a lot of us
    one cup for all mouths present
one great loaf
    for all
        one song on every lip
        one song, and the one cup
we men exchange a kiss, the women kiss
there is a slave among us, there's Erastus
(city treasurer) the ex-rabbi Crispus
        and Titius Justus multimillionaire
grains of wheat scattered in the fields
               joined in a single loaf
scattered at well or barracks or shop
    we meet on Saturdays at twilight
separate grapes joined in a single wine
           Irene moves among the tables
and we talk together, reclining,
until midnight, beneath the orange torches
what am I saying? until the Sunday dawns.

There is one we do not see, the one who presides
    He who was put to death, crowned with vine-shoots,
yes, we dine round a dead man
    this being a funeral feast. He
celebrated thus before he died, that we
    might be thus drawn together in his absence
("do this in memory of me")
    and in this wine he lives.
Dawn comes. The lights grow pale.
    "Good-by, Irene"
and in the misty streets we scatter
        yet remain united.

[R. P.-M.]

COPLAS ON THE DEATH OF MERTON

Our lives are rivers
that go to empty into the death
that is life
Your rather funny death Merton
    (or absurd like a koan?)
your General-Electric-brand death
and the corpse back to the U.S.A. in an Army plane
  with that sense of humor so much your own you must have laughed
you Merton now corpseless dying of laughter
I did too
The Dionysian initiates used to place ivy
  (I didn't know Death)
Today I joyfully type this word "death"
To die is not the same thing as a car wreck or
        a short circuit
  we have been dying all our lives
Confined within our lives
  like the worm in the apple? not
like the worm but like
the ripeness!
Or like mangoes in this Solentiname summer
yellowing, waiting for the
golden orioles . . .
      the hors d'oeuvres
in the restaurants were never the same
as they were advertised in the magazines
nor was the verse as good as we wanted it to be
or the kiss.
We have always wanted something beyond what we wanted
We are Somozas always wanting more and more haciendas
   *More More More**
not only more but also something different
    The wedding of desire
the coitus of perfect will is the act
of death.
    We walk about among things with the air

---

 * Italics indicate the use of English, French, or Latin in the original.—
D. D. W.

of having lost a most important
folder.
         We go up in elevators and we come down.
We go into supermarkets, into stores
like everybody else, looking for
a transcendental product.
                 We live as if waiting for an infinite
rendezvous. Or
           a telephone call from
the Ineffable.
And we are alone
immortal grains of wheat that do not die, we are alone.
We dream in steamer chairs on deck
   gazing at the daiquiri-colored sea
hoping that somebody will pass by and smile at us and
say *Hello*

Not sleep but lucidity.
   We move about in the traffic like sleepwalkers
     we pass by the lights
with eyes open and asleep
we sip a Manhattan as though asleep.
Not sleep
lucidity is the image of death
   of the illumination the blinding
radiance of death.
And it is not the Kingdom of Oblivion. Memory
  is the secretary of oblivion.
     She arranges the past in filing cabinets.
But when there is no more future but only a fixed present
all that we have lived comes to life again, no longer as memories
and reality reveals itself complete entire
in a *flash*.

Poetry too was a departure
like death. It had
the sadness of departing trains and planes
     Little Brenes Station
     in Cordobita la Llana
     the trains go by at night

46

"cante jondo" in the heart of Granada.
In all beauty, a sadness
and homesickness as in a foreign country
    MAKE IT NEW
   (a new heaven and a new earth)
but after that lucidity
you come back again to the clichés, the
slogans.
Only at moments when we are not being practical
concentrating on the Useless.   Real Gone
only then does the world open up for us.
Death is the act of total distraction
also: Contemplation.

Love, love above all, an anticipation
of death
   There was a taste of death in the kisses
     being
         is being
               in another being
   we exist only in love
But in this life we love only briefly
and feebly
   We love or exist only when we stop being
when we die
   nakedness of the whole being in order to make love
     make love not war
    that go to empty into the love
    that is life

The city descended from the heaven that is not Atlantic City
   And the Beyond is not an *American Way of Life*
      Retirement in Florida
or like an endless *Weekend.*
Death is a door opened
upon the universe
    There is no *NO EXIT* sign
and upon ourselves
   (to travel—
  upon ourselves—

not to Tokyo, Bangkok
        that's the *appeal*
    a *stewardess* in a kimono, *la cuisine*
continentale
that's the *appeal* of those Japan Air Line ads)
    A Wedding Night, said Novalis
It's not a Boris Karloff horror movie
And it's natural, like the fall of the apples
according to the law that attracts stars and lovers
There are no accidents
        just one more apple off the great Tree
you're just one more apple
Tom
        We leave our bodies as one leaves
        a motel room
But you're not Wells's *Invisible Man*
    Or like a ghost in an abandoned chalet
        We don't need *Mediums.*
And children know very well that death does NOT exist
that we are immortal
For can napalm kill life?
        From the gas chamber to nothingness?
    Or are the Gospels *science-fiction?*
Jesus entered the room and drove out the hired mourners
        That's why the swans sing said Socrates just
before they die
            Come, Caddo, we are all going up
                to the great Village
                to the great Village
Toward the place where all the buses and planes go
    And not as if to an end
    but to the Infinite
    we fly toward life with the speed of light
And like the fetus breaking the amniotic sac . . .
Or like cosmonauts . . .

                            the exit
                            from the chrysalis

    and it's a *happening.*
the *climax*
of life   *dies natalis*
    this prenatal life . . .

48

The matrix of matter abandoned
                              Not an absurdity:
                              but a mystery
a door opened upon the universe
and not upon the void
      (like the door of an elevator that wasn't there)
And by now they are definitive.
      . . . the same as waking up one morning
      to the voice of a nurse in a hospital
And we no longer have anything we just are
      we just exist and we are mere existence
                  The voice of the beloved speaking
                  my love, take off that *bra*
The opened door
that nobody can ever close again
            "God who bade us live"
even though we long to return to
      atomic linkings, to
            unconsciousness.
                  And the bombs bigger and bigger.
Necrophilia: flirtation with death. Passion for dead things
            (corpses, machines, money, dregs)
and if they dream about a woman they picture her
in a car.
      The irresistible fascination with the inorganic
            Hitler was seen in World War I
            ecstatic before a corpse
            refusing to move
(soldiers or machines, coins, crap)
Gas chambers by day and Wagner by night
"5 millions" said Eichmann (it was more like 6)
Or else we want to put make-up on the face of death
The Loved Ones (don't say the dead)
made up, manicured, smiling
in the Garden of Repose of Whispering Meadows
            cf. *THE AMERICAN WAY OF DEATH*
      A Martini or 2 to forget his face
relax & watch TV
            the pleasure of driving a Porsche
                  (*any line you choose*)
perhaps to wait for the resurrection frozen

in liquid nitrogen at $-197°$
   (put in storage like the grain that does not die)
until the day when immortality will come cheap
after coffee, Benedictine
a sport jacket to look young, to push death away
until they invent for us the serum of youth
     the antidote
for dying.
Like the good *cowboy* in the movies, who never dies.
  Looking in Miami for the Fountain of Youth.
After the advertised pleasures on the Virgin Islands.
Or on Onassis' yacht sailing on the Lethe . . .

You refused to be one of the men with a Name
and with a face that everybody recognizes in the pictures
in the papers
your desert that flourished like the lily was not that of
the *Paradise Valley Hotel*
    with cocktails at the pool
under the palm trees
nor were your solitudes those of *Lost Island*
  with the coconut palms bending over the sea
LOVE? It's in the movies
   The eruptions of eternity
   were brief
Those of us who haven't believed in the *Advertisements* of this world
   dinner for 2, *"je t'adore"*
     How to say love in Italian?
You told me: the
       Gospels don't mention contemplation.
Without LSD
but with the horror of God (or
    should we translate it rather as terror?)
   His love like the radiation that kills without touching us
and a void vaster than the Macrocosm!
   In your meditation you could see only that vision
   of the commercial plane from Miami to Chicago
   and the SAC plane with the Bomb inside
    the days when you were writing to me:
My life is one of deepening contradiction and frequent darkness

Your *Trip?* not at all interesting
    the journey to vast solitudes and extensions of nothingness
all as though made of plaster
                                    white and black, *with no color*
gazing at the luminous ball, blue and pink like agate
with Christmas on Broadway and copulation and songs
shimmering on the waves of the dusty Sea of Tranquillity
or the Sea of Crisis dead as far as the horizon. And
like a sparkling little ball on a *Christmas tree* . . .

    Time? *IS money*
it's *Time,* it's shit, it's nothing
    it's *Time* with a celebrity on the cover

And that ad for Borden's milk in the rain
years ago at Columbia, flashing on
and off, such fleeting flashes
        and the kisses in the movie theater
the films, the movie stars
so fleeting
        GONE WITH THE WIND
even though they still laugh beautiful and shining on the screen
the dead stars
    the car breaks down, the refrigerator
is going to be repaired
                        She was in a butter-yellow dress
                        orange-marmalade and strawberry-red
like a remembered ad in the *New Yorker*
and the *lipstick* smeared now with kisses
farewells at windows of planes that flew
            to oblivion
shampoos of girls more distant than the Moon
or than Venus
    A pair of eyes worth more than the Stock Exchange

Nixon's Inauguration Day is gone
the last TV image has dissolved
and they've swept up Washington
Time? Alfonso Time? *Is money* crap *shit*
time is the *New York Times* and *Time*
    And everything tasted like Coca-Cola . . .

Proteins and nucleic acids
"the beautiful numbers of their forms"
proteins and nucleic acids
the bodies feel like gas to the touch
beauty, like a bitter gas
tear gas
For the movie of this world is passing by . . .

like Coca-Cola
or copulation *for*
that matter
Our cells are as ephemeral as flowers
but not life
protoplasms, chromosomes but
not life
We shall live again the Comanches used to sing
our lives are rivers
that go to empty into life
now we see only through TV
then we shall see face to face
Every perception a rehearsal for death
beloved it is the time for pruning
All the kisses you couldn't give will be given
the pomegranates are in bloom
all love a *rehearsal* for death
So we fear beauty
When Li Chi was abducted by the Duke of Ch'in
she cried until she soaked her clothes
but in the palace she was sorry
she had wept.
The San Juan de la † is rounding the point
some ducks
swim by
"the uncanny isles"
or "desire" San Juan de la Cruz used to say
infinite desire
tears the fabric of this sweet encounter
and the Thracians used to weep at births says Herodotus
and sing at deaths
It was in Advent at Gethsemani when the apple trees

next to the greenhouse are like skeletons
with a blossoming of white ice like that
of the freezers.
I don't believe it Alfonso said to me in the Madhouse
when I told him that Pallais was dead
I think it's politics or
something like that.
Do they still bury a camel with them
for the journey? And in the Fiji Islands
clubs made of whale teeth?
Men's laughter at a joke is proof of their belief
in the resurrection
    or when a child cries in the strange night
and mamma calms him
Evolution is toward more life
    and it is irreversible
and incompatible with the hypothesis
of nothingness
"Ivy Mara ey"
looking for it they traveled as far as the interior of Brazil
("the land where no one ever died")
    Like mangoes in this Solentiname summer
ripening
while the Novitiate is over there under a hood of snow.
    The golden orioles fly
  to Deer Island where they sleep
you used to tell me
It is easy for us to approach Him
We are strangers in the cosmos like tourists
    we have no home here only hotels
Like gringo tourists
      everywhere
cameras clicking even strangers
    And as one leaves a motel room
      YANKI GO HOME
One more afternoon dies over Solentiname
Tom
      these sacred waters sparkle
and little by little they go out
it's time to light the Coleman lamp
    all joy is union

sorrow is to be without the others:
        Western Union
The cablegram from the Abbot of Gethsemani was yellow
   WE REGRET TO INFORM YOU etc. . . .
I just said
O.K.
       Where the dead unite and
            with the cosmos are
                  one
    because it is "far better" (Philippians *i*, 23)
As the moon dies and is born again . . .
    death is union and
       one is now oneself
         one is one with the world
death is far better
the malinches in bloom tonight, scattering their lives
    (their renunciation is a red flower)
death is union
    ½ moon over Solentiname
    with 3 men
one does not die alone
    (their Great Meeting Lodge) the Ojibwas
and the world is much more profound
Where the Algonquin spirits with spirit moccasins
hunt spirit beavers over the spirit snow
    we thought the moon was far away
to die is not to leave the world it is
to plunge into it
you are in the hidden part of the universe
   the *underground*
outside the *Establishment* of this world, outside of time-space
without Johnson or Nixon
   there are no tigers there
                 say the Malays
(an island of the West)
     that go to empty into the sea
     that is life
Where the dead gather O Netzahualcoyotl
or "Heart of the World"
   Hemingway, Raissa, Barth, Alfonso Cortés

the world is much more profound
     Hades, where Christ descended
       womb, belly (Matthew *xii,* 40)
        SIGN OF JONAS
   the depths of visible beauty
where swims the great cosmic whale
filled with prophets
     All the kisses you could not give will be given
One is transformed.
  . . . "as one was buried in one's mother's bosom . . ."
     a Cuna chief said to Keeler
Life does not end it is transformed
   another intrauterine state say the Koguis
that's why they bury them in hammocks
in the fetal position
   an ancient doctrine, said Plato
that off there in Hades there are
     people who have come from here . . .
Beziers, and the cathedral seen from the train
    Nothing of the yearned for has been lost
      the smell of the south of France
the red Tower of Saint Jacques by the Tarn
the lights of Paris white and green, and those of the Eiffel Tower:
    C-I-T-R-O-E-N
Lax has traveled with circuses
     and he knows what it means
  to strike the tent by lantern light
leaving the grounds deserted
and the truck ride by night toward another city
And when the wife of Chuang Tzu died
Chuang Tzu did not put on mourning
  Hui Tzu found him singing and dancing with
the rice pan for a tambourine
    the hammock is the placenta, the cord
of the hammock the umbilical cord
   "your headaches don't hurt you"
    seed-plant-seed
   the dialectic of destruction
     I mean
that of the wheat. To live

is to prepare for death and to give ourselves for the sowing of life
Until, masked and white-gloved, in comes
the agent
          of what Acronym we do not know
And to deliver ourselves to death with love
And
if the stars do not die
they are left alone
if the stars do not return to the cosmic dust
          seed, plant, seed
death is union
          not in *Junction City*
Or as the Cunas also say
          "some day we want to eat a good meal"
And we clamor for the surrender of the beloved
And as Abbot Hezekiah used to say: it is
(the frequent thought of death) "as
when in the calm sea the fishes play
and the dolphins leap for joy"
     And, as the moon dies . . .
          They are on an island, they told Columbus
     in Haiti, they are all on an island
          eating mamey fruit by night
Or Boluto Island, west of Tonga,
happy and covered with flowers and spiritual breadfruit
"It seems he was electrocuted"
                         Laughlin wrote me
"but at least it was quick"
                         broken the veil
that divides the soul and God . . . And:
. . . because love yearns for the act to be very brief . . .
     the rivers of love of the soul
     go there to enter the sea
she arrived beautiful as Joan Baez in her black car
You used to laugh at the ads in the *New Yorker*
     well here's one for Pan Am
     Ticket to Japan
                    To Bangkok
                         To Singapore
          All the way to the mysteries
A ticket to contemplation?

A ticket to contemplation.
                              And death.
            All the way to the mysteries
The commercial ads are
manuals of meditation, says Corita
                              Sister Corita
and ads of something more. Not to be taken
literally.
Biological death is a political matter
or something like that
        General Electric, the Parca
          a Vietnam *jet* for the corpse
but after this winter is gone, around Easter
or Whitsunday
you'll hear the Trappist tractors next to your cemetery
Trappist but noisy, turning over the earth
To sow, new Mayans, the ancient corn.
        The time of the resurrection of the *Caterpillars*
            and of the locusts
Like the banana tree that dies to give fruit the Hawaiians say.
        You were quite empty
            and having given all your love you had
nothing to give now
            And ready to go to Bangkok
in order to enter at the beginning of the new
to accept the death of the old
            Our lives
            that go to empty into life
the window of the great jet was weeping
            —as it took off from California—
        with joy!
At last you came to Solentiname (which wasn't *practical*)
after the Dalai Lama, and the Himalayas with their buses
painted like dragons
        to the "uncanny isles"; you are here
with your silent Tzus and Fus
Kung Tzu, Lao Tzu, Meng Tzu, Tu Fu, and Nicanor Parra
and everywhere; as simple to communicate with you
as with God (or as difficult)
        like the whole cosmos in a drop of dew
this morning on the way to the privy

Elijah snatched away by the chariot of cosmic energy
  and in the Papuan tribe when they saw the telegraph
  they made a tiny model of it
  so they could talk with the dead
The Celts used to lend money says Valerius Maximus
to be paid beyond the grave.

  All the kisses given or not given.
That's why the swans sing said Socrates
upon your chest the fan still
turning
    We love or are only when we die.
  The great final act the gift of one's whole being.
O.K.

  [K. R. and M. J.-F.]

  Note: Jorge Manrique's *Coplas en la muerte de su padre* ("Verses on the Death of His Father"), written in 1476, is one of the greatest poems in Spanish, a lament not only for the death of Manrique's father but for the passing of his whole era, the Spanish Middle Ages. In his *Coplas* Cardenal consciously echoes Manrique's opening lines: "Nuestras vidas son los ríos / que van a dar en el mar, / que es el morir." ("Our lives are the rivers / that go to empty into the sea, / which is death")—D. D. W.

LORDS DEFENDERS OF LAW AND ORDER (PSALM 57)

Lords defenders of Law and Order:
Your justice is it not perhaps class justice?
  Civil Courts to protect private property
  Criminal Courts to dominate the dominated
The freedom you talk about is freedom for capital
  your "free world" means freedom to exploit
Your law is the shotgun and your order the jungle
  you own the police
  you own the judges
There are no landowners or bankers in your jails.

The bourgeois begins to go astray at his mother's breast
he has class prejudices from the day he's born
   like the rattlesnake he's born with his poison sac
   like the tiger shark he's born a man-eater

O God put an end to the status quo
      tear out the fangs of the oligarchs
Let them be flushed away like the water in the basin
   let them wither like weeds beneath the weed-killer

They are the "worms" when the Revolution comes
They are not body cells but microbes
   Miscarriages of the new man, they must be cast out
Before they bear thorns let the tractor uproot them

The common man will take his ease in the exclusive clubs
he will take over private enterprises
the just man will rejoice in the People's Courts
We shall celebrate in spacious squares the anniversary of
         the Revolution
   The God that exists is the God of the common man

                                        [D. D. W.]

RECORDINGS OF THE SACRED PIPE

Things that now only Black Elk knew
and has wished to have recorded
      what was learned from Elk Head
another old man of the tribe. . . To transmit it
to the new youths
   the knowledge of the sacred pipe

"It is called a peace pipe, but now
there is no peace in the world" says Black Elk
"not even among neighbors, and from
what I've been told, there has not for a long time been any peace
      in the world"

59

The pipe is passed around.
  (Not only among men
    also inside men
  and also peace among the other creatures)
The Hut represents the universe and
the center pole, Wakan-tanka,
who holds up the universe.
The earth that she gave to men is red
the men who live on the earth are red
each red dawn a sacred event
  the earth, sacred
      and every step on it
        like a prayer.
The pipe is passed around
in the smoke the earth ascends, this great island,
the animals with four feet and the animals with wings.
The pipe is the universe; and it is man.
One smokes: and it enters into the center of the universe
    and into oneself.
Elk Head was talking
of the kinship among all the creatures of the universe
and the kinship between mankind and Wakan-tanka.
The tepee is the world
the fire inside the tepee Wakan-tanka,
who is at the center of the world.
      Nomads on the prairies, they put
      Wakan-tanka's tepee in the center of the camp.
Also: the tepee is the universe and
around the tepee: the infinite, Wakan-tanka.
Poles of young willow trees
because as the leaves of the willow trees fall
and are reborn
so men die and come to life again.
He inhales the pipe and says:
"Let our brothers be gentle and not fear us."

The messages usually come in the shape of an animal
at times a very small one, an ant.
Animals are important, wise in their own right.
Black Elk says in an off-hand way:
  "It is no accident

that we have two feet like the birds."
The drum, round, is the universe. And its one-note sound
the beating of the heart of the universe.
The Sun Dance, with an eagle feather:
the feather, Wakan-tanka, who lives in the blue.
The Dance takes place in the full moon
    (the moon waxes and wanes, like our ignorance, that comes
        and goes).
The face, painted red: the red represents
all that is sacred, especially the earth
    from where the bodies come,
and to where the bodies return.
A black circle around the face
because Wakan-tanka is like a circle, she has no end.
There is much power in a circle
birds that fly in circles know this
    and their houses are circles
the coyotes who live in round hollows know this.

He said: "I was five years old when I began to hear voices.
Now I see everything from the peak of old age
bent over by these years as by a heavy snow:
    Many made into grass in the prairies . . .
It was in the Moon of the Strawberries (May)
and the *wasichus* found much yellow metal,
Crazy Horse was twenty and Red Cloud was the Chief.
My mother used to say: 'If you don't behave the *wasichus* will
        carry you off.'
"It was at the end of the Moon of Ripe Cherries (July)
and us children were playing the game of Knock-Them-off-the-Horse.
In my tepee I could hear the coyotes calling to the stars.
    My mother bent over the fire, roasting buffalo.
    My father arrives at night, on his shoulders an antelope.
"I see from my old age as from a lonely hill
        the stagecoaches in a circle
        our men going around in another circle
        closer and closer
        and then going around in two circles
        in opposite directions
        lying flat on our horses
            firing underneath their necks."

A leather half-moon,
    the moon represents all the things
that live and die.
They cut out another circle and they paint it red
and it is the earth. (It is sacred
because on it men place their feet
and raise their voices to Wakan-tanka.
She is of the family of mankind, they call her Mother.)
Blue Whirlwind breaks in: "The prayer
    a prayer of all things
because all things are really one.
We always see the sacred sky
and we know what it is and what it represents.
To know the four Beings of the universe
is to know that they are really One.
The sky is a shawl that enfolds the universe
and also enfolds the man who talks to Wakan-tanka."
And Black Elk adds: "Perhaps you have noticed
    that even though the breeze is very slight
    you can always hear the voice of the poplar."

First (and most important) is peace inside you
when you feel your kinship with the universe
and you feel Wakan-tanka in the center of the universe
and that the center is everywhere and inside you
the second peace is between two men and the third between
        two peoples
but there is none between peoples if there is none inside of man.

"In the Moon of the Yellow Leaves (September)
they signed a treaty with Red Cloud.
In the Moon of the Falling of the Leaves (October)
we camped near the Black Hills.
Much bison and we ate much meat and tanned much leather.
Crazy Horse wanted nothing to do with the *wasichus*.
In the Moon of the Birth of Grass (March)
there was a great council with the *wasichus*.
Crazy Horse and Sitting Buffalo did not attend.
Words and words and words: like a wind . . .
The Great Father in Washington wanted the Black Hills.

They would be like snow melting in the hands.
I was sad . . . It was so joyful to play there
and people were always happy in the Black Hills.
    And I remembered my vision
how I was carried there to the center of the world.
In the Moon of the Ripe Plums (August)
began the scattering of our people.
We burned the grass behind us
the smoke broad as the sky
      the glow broad as the night.
Sitting Bull went to Grandmother Earth (Canada)
Crazy Horse refused to leave the earth that was ours."

The ball, painted red (the color of the world)
with a blue circle (the color of the sky)
(Heaven and Earth come together in the ball)
the ball is very sacred, a little girl throws the ball
because she is new-come from Wakan-tanka.
She throws the ball in the four directions
because Wakan-tanka is in all directions.
The little girl's ball falls on the people
(like the power of Wakan-tanka on the people)
The buffaloes could not play this game
and they gave it to the two-footed ones.
The pipe goes round.
Brave Buffalo says: "One must have
a favorite animal. Study it
    know its movements and its sounds.
They want to communicate with man."
The pipe with red-willow bark.
   The great visions are for the whole nation.

"We learned in the Moon of the Falling of the Leaves
that the Black Hills had been sold.
One night, very cold, fire all night
I heard a little noise outside the tepee
I went out and it was a pair of porcupines
huddled together in spite of their quills
and we didn't scare them away because we were so sorry for them.
At the end of the Moon of the New Calves (April)

they took us to the fort. Crazy Horse surrendered
I saw him take off his war feathers
        he sat upon the ground.
They put us on islands to live like *wasichus*.
I did not tell anybody about my vision.
    I could not do anything because I was a child
    and not even Sitting Bull had done anything.
Lying in my bison-skin cloak I heard a coyote far off
I knew he was saying something, he wasn't saying words
        something clearer than words.
And strange news from the west:
Jack Wilson to the *wasichus* (but Wowoka was his name)
he saw the world all new, where everyone was alive
and the slaughtered bison ran again:
In the next Moon of the Birth of Grass
it would be the new earth, the return of the bison.
    The winter was very cold like a single long night.
The coyotes outside in the frozen night made me afraid.
And I remembered Crazy Horse.
In that Moon of the Snow upon the Tepee (December)
the *wasichus* killed the last of the bison.
No one knows where Crazy Horse is buried
        no matter: he is grass."

Lively Sparrowhawk says:
"Part of the plant goes up and welcomes the sun
and the other goes down seeking the water.
Wakan-tanka teaches the birds to make their nests
yet not all the nests are alike.
There are animals content with very bad houses
others have pretty ones.
Since I was a child I have observed the leaves of the trees
I have never seen two alike
if you look closely: there are little differences . . ."

And Blue Whirlwind:
"Some people prefer to be alone, away from the others.
With closed eyes many things can be seen
but these things are also distracting.
Some look for a hill, there they close their eyes.
Men are not enough, and one seeks an animal.

You can learn from animals' ways. For example:
horses get restless before a storm."
And again Brave Buffalo: "I was 10 years old
I asked the trees, the thickets.
   It seemed to me that the flowers were looking at me.
The muddy stones: some with faces like men
none of them answered me.
In a dream a round stone answered me
it said: Wakan-tanka.
It's curious: there are certain stones on high hills
round as the sun and the moon.
We know that all round things are relatives.
Those stones have stayed a long time looking at the sun.
I can't talk to Wakan-tanka, and I talk to stones."

And from Black Elk this prayer: "You placed
the four directions in the form of a cross.
The good road and the hard one you made them cross
and there where they cross the place is sacred."

Wounded Knee saw: bodies upon the snow
   a baby nursing at the breast of its dead mother.
From the summit of the mountain of old age
he sees again the bodies upon the snow
as clearly as he saw it all with young eyes, and he sees
. that something else died there, in the mud of snow and blood
and was buried by that great snow that fell:
a very beautiful dream.
(And strange news from the west:
      under a rainbow tepees of clouds
many many camping in a great circle
around green grass happy horses
animals of all kinds on green hills
and the hunters came with game singing.)
      There was now no center anywhere.
      The sacred tree was dead.
Now he leaves his old voice on a recorder.

"When I was 20 in the Moon of the Yellow Leaves
I went off to the circus with Long Hair (Buffalo Bill)
to learn the secrets of the *wasichus*.

On the road-of-iron, to the great city
of lights so bright you couldn't see the stars
they told me they came from the power of the thunder
there I went like one who has never had a vision.
     I saw nothing that would help my people
they took things away from one another, the *wasichus,*
they didn't know that the earth was their mother."

He ended saying: "In these sad days
sad for my people
we are fighting each other for the ball
and some do not even take an interest in picking up the ball
this makes me weep.
     But soon they are going to pick up the ball
and the ball is going to come back to the center
and our people will be in the center with the ball."

And again, on the reservation:
     "There is no strength in a square"
(on the Pine Ridge Reservation
          in the square houses of the whites)
"You have seen that everything the Indians make is in a circle
and it's because the Mystery makes everything in circles
and all things try to be round
          the sky is round
and I have heard that the earth is like a ball
          the very strong wind goes in whirls
birds make their nests in the shape of a circle
because they have the same religion as we do
the sun and the moon swing in circles
and they both have a round shape
the seasons end where they begin
just like the life of man
our tepees were round like nests
and placed in the shape of a circle
now they have put us in square boxes."
     The vision was true, he says.
Almost blind. Surrounded by treeless hills.
(Not even a cloud)
"Great Spirit more ancient than all need,

than all prayer
          hear my fading voice!"
(Not even one cloud—
    the old men could not remember a greater drought)
"I send you my voice through a people in despair.
You told me that it would make the tree blossom.
With tears on my face Great Spirit
with tears on my face I come to tell you now
that the tree never blossomed!"
(The sky was still without a cloud)
"I am old, you can see, I went away and I did nothing. Here
in the center of the world, where as a child I had the vision
here I am again and the tree is withered.
Again, and perhaps this is the last time
I remember the vision. Perhaps a tiny root is living
feed it then if this is so, let it have leaves
and flowers and birds that sing.
Listen to me so that they may enter again into the hoop
and find the good road that is red
and the tree of the great shade!"
(In the sky, a few clouds
afterward a rain . . . a drizzle
    a muffled thunder)
The saintly redskin with tears on his face:
"In my sadness
hear me in my sadness
for perhaps I nevermore never again will speak:
            let my people live."
He fell silent. The tears smearing the paint
the tears and the rain smearing the paint
(soon afterward
    the sky clear again)

    The ball will come back to the center:
    and they in the center with the ball.

                [D. D. W.]

THE ARRIVAL

We get off the plane and we go, Nicaraguans and foreigners,
all mixed together toward the huge lighted building—first stop
Immigration and Customs—and as we approach, passport in hand,
I think of how proud I am to be holding
the passport of my socialist country, and of my satisfaction
at arriving in a Socialist Nicaragua. "Comrade"
they'll say to me—a revolutionary comrade welcomed
by the revolutionary comrades of Immigration and Customs—
not that there won't be controls; there must be controls
so that capitalism and Somozaism never come back—
and the emotion of coming back to my country during a revolution
with more changes, more and more decrees
of expropriation that I'd hear of, changes more and more radical,
many surprises in the short time I've been away
and I see joy in the eyes of everybody—the ones that have stayed,
the others are gone already—and now we go into the brightness
and they ask natives and foreigners for their passports . . .
but it was all a dream and I am in Somoza's Nicaragua
and they take away my passport with the icy courtesy
with which Security would tell me "Please come in"
and they take the passport inside and they don't bring it back (surely
they must surely be phoning Security
or the Presidential Palace or somebody or other) and by now
all the other passengers are gone and I don't know if I'll be arrested
but no: at the end of an hour they come back with my passport.
The CIA must have known that this time I didn't go to Cuba
and that I was just a single day in East Berlin,
and so at last I can go through Customs
all alone in Customs with my ancient suitcase
and the kid that inspects just pretends to inspect
without inspecting anything and he murmurs to me: "Father"
and he doesn't dig deep down into the suitcase where he would find
the phonograph record with Allende's last appeal to the people
from the Palace, interrupted by the sound of bombs exploding,
the record I bought in East Berlin, or Fidel's speech
about Allende's overthrow, the one Sergio gave me,
and the kid says: "It's eight o'clock already and we haven't had supper,
us customs workers get hungry, too."

"What time do you have your supper?" I asked "Not till after the last
    plane lands"
and now I'm moving toward the dark demolished city
where everything is just the same and nothing's going on but I
    have seen
his eyes and with his eyes he has said to me: "Comrade."

[D. D. W.]

CONDENSATIONS–AND A VISION IN SAN JOSÉ DE COSTA RICA

Up there the stars are calling,
inviting us to wake up, to evolve,
    to come out into the cosmos.
They begotten by pressure and heat.
    Like bright boulevards lit up
    or towns seen by night from a plane.
    Love: that lit the stars . . .
The universe is made of union.
    The universe is condensation.
Condensation is union, and it is heat. (Love)
The universe is love.
    An electron never wants to be alone.
Condensation, union, that's what the stars are.
The Law of Gravity
    che muove il sole e l'altre stelle
is an attraction between bodies, and the attraction
is quickened when the bodies come closer.
The force of attraction of chaotic matter.
    Each molecule
attracts every other molecule in the universe.
    The straightest line is a curve.
    Only love is revolutionary.
    Hatred is always reactionary.
Heat is a stirring (agitation) of the molecules
as love is a stirring (and as love is heat).

An electron seeks to belong to a complete group or a subgroup.
    All matter is attraction.
The electrons of the atom spin in elliptic orbits
as the planets spin in elliptic orbits
(and love follows elliptic orbits).
Each one of the molecules of the earth attracts
the moon, the sun, and the stars.
It has rained in the night and the toads are croaking
in the moonlight, croaking for the females, calling them
to copulation.
    And the atoms, the loving atoms join
    until so many atoms have united
    that they start to shine and it's a star.
(What happens in sexual union? And how does it produce
new life?) And from the stars came the dance.
Among stalactites and stalagmites (in the last gallery)
a bison modeled in clay from the cave itself
mounting a female modeled with the same clay
and on the floor footprints, in the clay soles and heels
of adolescents from the ice age who danced
and danced before the bisons.
    The dance that was learned from the stars.

Sunday night, and on Wall Street a filthy wind
blows newspapers along the empty sidewalk. Wall Street, star-lit,
ghostly, and empty. The bank windows dark,
but not all of them. Some rows are lit up
in the black bulks. They can be identified:
the foreign trade departments of the great banks.
The iron doors locked and barred.
But through back doors some people have gone into
the foreign trade departments. Lights secret meetings
decisions unknown to us (and like the shares up goes
the smoke of their Havana cigars) but they affect us all.
A riot in Malaysia over devaluation, buses burned
and blood flows in the street like water from a hydrant.
At the hour when stars shine over Wall Street
and at the hour when banks open in London.

Matter attracts matter
and as condensation increases, its power

of attraction increases. Under equal conditions
a condensation two million miles in diameter
exerts twice as much attraction as one of a single million. So
the greater the condensation the greater its possibility
of growing more bringing together minor condensations.
Now let us suppose that an enormous mass of uniform gas
spreads in space for millions and millions of miles
in all directions: any slight alteration
in its uniformity can unleash condensations and
condensations, of any imaginable dimension.

Capitalism will pass away. You will no longer see the Stock Market.
"As sure as spring follows winter . . ."
     My Vision in San José de Costa Rica.
And if "the last enemy to be destroyed will be death"
before that, selfishness will be destroyed.
As different from present-day man as he is from Peking Man.

    Competition prevents cooperation.
There is separation between man and man.
A divided humanity.
      The first fish
died of suffocation. The first fish that leaped to the land
was like Che.
         But others followed later on.

Anyone would think that a small disturbance
that affects only a small mass of gas
would produce a condensation of small proportions.
But the gravitation of the smallest body
has repercussions throughout the universe. The moon
creates tides on the earth and on the most distant stars.
When the baby throws his toy on the floor
he perturbs the movement of all the stars in the universe.
As long as gravitation exists, no
perturbation can remain confined
to an area less than the totality of space.

"The attempt to climb to the assault of Heaven," said Lenin
Lenin no less (the Paris Commune)
    Communal and personal, classless and stateless.

A new man with new chromosomes.
It is easy to produce and distribute what we need
    on this celestial body
(economics isn't anything complicated).
    The more violent the perturbation,
the more intense will be the condensations
but even the most insignificant one develops
condensations even though they are of extremely weak intensity
and we have already seen that the fate of a condensation
is determined not by its intensity but by its mass.
However weak their original intensity may have been
the great condensations gradually become greater
and greater, and the small ones disappear, absorbed
by the greater ones, and finally there is left only a collection
of enormous condensations. Like them are the phenomena that we call
socializations, and like them is
        the Revolution.

The universe is homogeneous. The fragments of stars
in the South Kensington Geological Museum
show that they are of the same flesh as ours.
    (We too are star.)
"Celestial flesh," said Rubén.
    We too are children of the sun
(the heat of our blood is solar heat)
    begotten by the stars!
"Honey, I'm happy in the mountains
because I'm on my people's battlefront."

    And the battle is already twenty billion years old.
But: "the Revolution does not end in this world"
if we do not conquer death
    the status quo ultimately triumphs
        death is the status quo.

And my Vision in San José de Costa Rica (I shall tell
of my Vision): in a taxi at night
having just arrived by plane to attend a Congress of Writers,
my Vision was: neon signs, drugstores, autos,
boys on motorcycles, gas stations, bars, people on the sidewalks,

a bunch of girls in uniform, workers in groups,
   and I saw everything organized through love.
The color of a sweater spoke to me of love,
love moved the cars, lit up those lights—all of them.
The fashions of the girls, what were they but love,
   the neighborhood kids, united by love
and through love were planted trees with red flowers
   a long-haired boy—his hair long through love
an ad: IMPERIAL. Who knows what it is but it must be
something to share, something to give to someone.
A telephone booth and somebody phoning somebody or other.
Mother and child along the street and there is another love,
   a couple goes by hugging, another love,
     a pregnant woman almost screaming love.
My taxi goes on. Two people standing on a sidewalk: one telling
    a story
(they must be friends)
       A very handsome animal is man, I say to myself
Fried Chicken, Pastry Shop . . . that's also love.
Someone in a great hurry—arriving late—Where? For a date
or a party or a house where he loves someone.
Another one carrying bread. To share with others. Communion.
Brightly lit restaurants: they also are for union,
PILSEN Beer: it also announces association, gathering together
   Coca-Cola
(what crap) but tonight the sign spells out:
           C o m m u n i o n
A beautiful species I said, how I love it
   all born from copulation
     born for love
(in one neighborhood a house with a little party. How nice!)
And I saw that it was wonderful to die for others.
That was my Vision, that night in San José de Costa Rica:
all of creation even on the billboards was groaning in pain
because of man's exploitation of man. All of creation
   was screaming, screaming with great shouts for
the Revolution.

    [D. D. W.]

IDENTIFICATIONS

Here are my attempts, with help from Father Cardenal, to satisfy the curious reader. I apologize for any curiosity left unsatisfied.—D. D. W.

Alfonso: see Cortés, Alfonso.

Algonquin: a group of Indian tribes whose territory extended from Labrador to the Rocky Mountains.

Allende Gossens, Salvador (1909–73): Chile's Marxist president, killed in a military coup.

The American Way of Death: Nancy Mitford's 1963 satire on the ascendancy of the mortician.

Arango, Gonzalo: contemporary Colombian poet, founder of the *nadaísta* (nihilist) movement.

Báez Bone, Adolfo: Nicaraguan, a close friend of Cardenal, killed in guerrilla fighting.

Barth, Karl (1886–1968): Swiss theologian, a leader of German opposition to Hitler.

Béziers: a French city on the Mediterranean.

Brenes: an Andalusian town mentioned in a song.

Caddo: a group of American Indian tribes.

cante jondo (deep song): Andalusian gypsy music.

Castillo y Guevara, Sor Josefa del: seventeenth-century Colombian mystic.

ceiba: the silk-cotton tree.

Che: Ernesto Che Guevara (1927–67), Argentine doctor and Cuban revolutionary, whose nickname was Che.

che muove il sole e l'altre stelle ("that moves the sun and the other stars"): from the last line of Dante's *Paradiso*: *l'amor que muove il sole e l'altre stelle*.

chilán: Mayan soothsayer.

Ch'in, Duke of: a Chinese personage in an anecdote told by Chuang-Tzu.

74

Chuang-Tzu: a fourth-century B.C. Chinese mystic and philosopher. One of Merton's books is *The Way of Chuang-Tzu.*

Comanche: a Shoshonean Indian tribe in southwestern United States.

Cordobita la Llana: an Andalusian town mentioned in a song.

Corita: see Kent, Corita.

Cortés, Alfonso: a mad Nicaraguan poet whom Cardenal knew as a young man and whose poetry was translated by Merton.

Cuautla: a city in the Mexican State of Morelos, near Cuernavaca.

Cuernavaca: capital of the Mexican State of Morelos, where Cardenal studied for the priesthood.

Cunas: an Indian tribe living on the San Blas Islands in the Caribbean and in Panama and Colombia.

Darío, Rubén (1867–1916): Nicaragua's first great poet, founder of *modernismo,* and the most influential Hispanic poet of his time.

dies natalis: birthday.

Drake, Sir Francis (1540?–96): navigator and privateer, first Englishman to circumnavigate the globe, plunderer of Spanish ships and cities in the West Indies, and one of the officers who helped defeat the Spanish Armada in 1588.

Eichmann, Adolf (1906–62): Hitler's master murderer, under whose direction between five and six million Jews were slaughtered.

Gethsemani, Kentucky: a Trappist monastery where Cardenal became a novice in 1957 under the supervision of Thomas Merton.

Gone with the Wind: Margaret Mitchell's enormously popular post-Civil-War Southern romance, awarded the Pulitzer Prize in 1937.

González, Fernando: twentieth-century Colombian mystic and radical.

gusano (worm): any antirevolutionary.

Hawkins, Sir John (1532–95): English naval officer and slave trader, in command of a squadron in the defeat of the Spanish Armada in 1588.

Hui Tzu: a logician who was Chuang Tzu's close friend and constant opponent.

insulas extrañas: a reference to a verse by the Spanish mystic poet San Juan de la Cruz.

Jonas: Jonah. See entries under Matthew and Merton.

Karloff, Boris: stage name of William Henry Pratt (1887–1969), British actor who was featured in American horror films.

katún: Mayan cycle of 7,200 days (20 years), named after its final day. Since the Spaniards arrived in the first year of Katún 11 Ahau (1541), this is a symbol of recurring misfortune.

Keeler, Clyde E.: author of *Secrets of the Cuna Earth Mother.*

Kent, Corita (1918–): painter and serigrapher, formerly a nun.

Koan: in Zen Buddhism, a nonsensical question addressed to a student, who must supply an answer, in the hope that his meditation on the question will be illuminating.

Kogui: Indians of the Sierra de Santa Marta in Colombia.

Kung Tzu: a Chinese author mentioned by Merton.

Lao-tzu: Chinese philosopher, sixth-century B.C., reputed founder of Taoism.

Laughlin, James (1914–): poet and publisher of New Directions, friend of Merton and Cardenal.

Li Chi: a character in a story by Chuang Tzu.

The Loved One: Evelyn Waugh's 1948 satire on American glorification of the dead.

Luke *xvi,* 9: "And I say unto you, make to yourselves friends of worldly wealth; that, when ye fail, they may receive you into everlasting habitations."

malinche: a tropical tree.

Managua: capital of Nicaragua and one of its largest lakes.

Maritain, Raïsa (1883–): wife of Jacques Maritain (1882–1973), famous French philosopher and convert to Catholicism. Merton admired them both.

Matthew *xii,* 40: "For as Jonas was three days and three nights in the whale's belly; so shall the Son of Man be three days and three nights in the heart of the earth."

Meng-tsu (ca. 380–289 B.C.): Chinese philosopher, also known as Mencius.

Merton, Thomas (1915–68): American poet-priest, under whose guidance Cardenal was a Trappist novice. Author of *The Way of Chuang Tzu* and *The Sign of Jonas,* a spiritual diary. He was accidentally electrocuted on December 10, 1968, in Bangkok.

milpa: cornfield.

Netzahaualcóyotl (1402–72): poet-philosopher who was King of Texcoco.

Novalis: pseudonym of Baron Friedrich von Hardenburg (1772–1801), a leader among early German romantic poets. His best-known work, a prose poem, *Hymmen an die Nacht* ("Hymn to Night"), was inspired by the death of his fiancée.

Ojibwas: North American Indians near Lake Superior.

Pallais: a Nicaraguan poet-priest.

Parra, Nicanor (1914–): Chilean poet and physicist, author of *Poems and Antipoems* and *Emergency Poems*.

Pasos, Joaquín: twentieth-century Nicaraguan vanguard poet who died young.

Petén: forest and lake (Petén Itzá) in northern Guatemala where Mayan ruins are found.

Philippians *i*, 23, 24: "For I am in a strait betwixt two, having a desire to depart, and to be with Christ; which is far better. Nevertheless, to abide in the flesh is more needful for you."

Popo: Popocatépetl, extinct Mexican volcano.

Propertius, Sextus (*ca.* 50–15 B.C.): Roman elegiac love poet, one of a group, including Ovid and Virgil, patronized by Maecenas.

quetzal: a handsome long-tailed golden-green and scarlet bird, the national bird of Guatemala, also the Guatemalan unit of currency.

Quetzalcóatl: the feathered serpent god in Aztec and Toltec mythology.

Rubén: see Darío, Rubén.

Saint Jacques: a town in the south of France, mentioned in Merton's *The Seven Storey Mountain*.

San Juan de la Cruz (1542–91): Spanish mystic and theologian, friend of Santa Teresa de Jesús.

The Sign of Jonas: see Merton.

Solentiname, Nuestra Señora de: Father Cardenal's commune on Mancarrón, largest island of the Solentiname Archipelago, in Lake Nicaragua.

Somoza García, Anastasio (Tacho) (1896–1956): dictator of Nicaragua for twenty years until his assassination, when his son Luis became president. Since 1967 Anastasio Somoza Debayle (Tachito), Luis's brother, has been in power.

Tachito and Tacho: see Somoza.

Tarn: a river in southern France.

Tonga: a group of South Pacific Islands.

Tu Fu (712–70): Chinese poet-philosopher mentioned by Merton.

Valerius Maximus (first century A.D.): Roman consul, historian, and rhetorician.

Wakan-tanka: the Great Spirit of the Dakota Indians.

wasichu: an Indian term for the white man.

Wells, Herbert George (1866–1946): British novelist and sociologist. His *The Invisible Man*, a fantasy, was published in 1897.

Yvy Mara ey: Land without Evil (Paradise) in the Guaraní language.

zapote: the sapodilla tree of tropical America.